TEMPTATION AND TESTING

TEMPTATION AND TESTING

Paul Butler

First published in Great Britain in 2007

Society for Promoting Christian Knowledge
36 Causton Street
London SW1P 4ST

British Library Cataloguing-in-Publication Data
A catalogue record for this book is available from the British Library

ISBN 978–0–281–05840–2

1 3 5 7 9 10 8 6 4 2

Typeset by Graphicraft Ltd, Hong Kong
Printed in the UK by CPI Bookmarque, Croydon, CR0 4TD

To Mum and Dad
without whose loving care
I would not be the person I am

Contents

Preface

This book began life as a series of talks given during Lent 2004 in Dibden Purlieu and Throop, Bournemouth. It was the encouragement of some who attended these that first led to turning them into a book. At times it has been a real struggle to transform them into the form in which they now appear. I have constantly had to tussle with the question of how much I reveal of myself and my own life. I have a responsibility not to cast others in a poor light, but how much truth about myself dare I reveal? I hope that as you read you will feel that I have been honest and open enough to be of help and value to all who read.

I am deeply grateful to my very astute daughter Caroline who had the courage to be the first reader of the manuscript. Her comments were very helpful. She assures me that she was not too shocked by what she discovered about her father in these pages. But she does think some readers will, but should not, be shocked. 'You are, after all, just human like the rest of us, Dad. But some seem to think bishops are slightly different.'

I am very grateful for those who have encouraged me to return to book writing, in particular my former colleague Dave Welch. Alongside Dave, Nigel Anstey, Alison Kennedy, Ola Franklin, Andy Campbell, Steven Saxby, Sarah Hayward (née Batson) and Cathie Smith were wonderful colleagues and encouragers in ministry; I owe to all of them and earlier colleagues in Walthamstow – Rosie Eager, Linda Scott, David Coring, Michael Reeves, Jeremy Alcock and Roy Foreman – far more than I could ever express adequately. The people of Walthamstow, in the four churches I served, our neighbouring church communities and the wider community, have, however, made the biggest impact of all.

Since moving to the Diocese of Winchester I have been enormously helped and encouraged by many people. I am indebted to you all for keeping the teaching of God's Word at the top of my agenda.

Alison Barr has been wonderful as editor; her initial encouragement to turn the talks into a book was crucial as was her advice about its structure. It has been a privilege to work with Alison again after a few years' gap.

I am, however, most grateful to my fabulous family, Rosemary, Caroline, David, Andrew and Sarah, who bring so much joy into my life – and who most often see and have to put up with this frail human who regularly gives in to temptation and fails the tests but who has discovered God's amazing forgiving, renewing grace. Thank you – you are brilliant!

A note on the ideas for reflection

At the end of each chapter there is a section with ideas for reflection. These can be used individually by the reader. They have been designed so that they could also be used by a group. The contents of the chapter should provoke questions for discussion but some suggested questions are offered as an aid to this. There are also suggestions made about a picture, which may aid discussion or quiet reflection. The pictures by Dinah Roe Kendall are from her book *Allegories of Heaven* (Piquant Publishing). The pictures by Sidney Spencer are those from his series 'Christ in the Wilderness'; they can be found in *Stanley Spencer* by Keith Bell (Phaidon Press). The Jesus Mafa pictures are by a Cameroonian artist and can be viewed on the web at <www.jesusmafa.com>; copies can be purchased via the website. The prayers are mainly written in the first person singular but can easily be used by a group changing this to the first person plural.

1

It happens to us all

———◆———

I had arrived in Edinburgh on an early flight ready to take part in the Make Poverty History Rally. The streets were still very quiet, though everywhere there were signs of the preparations being made for this historic day; crush barriers, some shops sadly boarded up, banners being erected, and TV and radio crews setting up their satellite communications systems and a growing number of people in the official white T-shirts. The sun was shining brightly and Edinburgh looked wonderful. I was walking along Princes Street on my way to the ecumenical service being held at the Methodist Central Hall, Tollcross.

As I turned into Lothian Road I saw just a few yards ahead a *Big Issue* seller. I knew what to expect as it had happened many times before. As I drew closer the magazine was politely held out towards me and the young man's voice gently enquired, '*Big Issue*, sir?' Our brains and emotions work incredibly fast and the range of thoughts that had gone through my mind over the past few yards were legion. Then out of my mouth I heard myself respond, 'It's okay, I've already got one.' He smiled and I walked on.

Whatever had possessed me to lie to this man? Here I was wearing my purple bishop's shirt, collar in, cross around my neck, on the way to pray and worship as a prelude to demonstrating with 220,000 others for justice for the poor – and I had chosen to lie! I could have stopped and bought a copy (a fairly regular practice for me) or I could have politely declined. But for some reason I had chosen to try and make myself appear good by saying that I had already bought a copy – when I simply hadn't. Did I want to appear holy? Probably that was part of the reason behind the response. Did I want to avoid appearing mean or uninterested by declining to buy? That, I am sure, was also part of what was going on inside me. I could analyse it even more but that would only be to offer excuses.

The simple fact is that I chose to lie. The temptation to appear to be good led me into an act of falsehood, and thus sin. I wish I had acted differently, but I did not. I had shocked myself by my response. Indeed I would go so far as to say that by the time I had reached the Central Hall I was disgusted with myself. So, when it came to saying the Lord's Prayer in the service, I found it meaningful to pray, 'Forgive us our sins' as I could recognize where I had failed, yet again. Along with everyone else gathered there I came to the foot of the cross of Jesus and asked for God, in his loving mercy, to forgive me. On this particular day, as I prayed these very familiar words, I had a deep sense of God's wonderful forgiveness of me. Sometimes that sense comes slowly, even very slowly, as I wrestle with my guilt but on this day it came flooding in; I knew God had graciously forgiven me, yet again.

It is very simple to trivialize the question of temptation. The marketing and advertising industries are particularly good at doing so. Many years ago there was a series of adverts for cream cakes under the catch phrase, 'Naughty, but nice'. In one simple phrase the slogan writer had captured the idea of something being 'wrong' or 'bad for us' while also being pleasurable and joyful. Arguably the whole advertising industry is based on 'tempting' us into buying products that we do not really want, or need. A recent estimate suggested that there is, for example, £200 million worth of unused fitness equipment in the lofts, garages, sheds and cellars of the United Kingdom. All was presumably bought in response to adverts and advice about health and fitness. Most was probably bought with the very best of intentions. But it lies idle. When a new Aldi's store opened in my home town of Romsey my whole family enjoyed many products in their range of foods available under the brand name, 'Temptation'.

Now overeating, and the related concern of obesity, are serious matters in the Western world – so perhaps 'Temptation' is not such a bad title for a range of foods that we could all happily live without. But temptation is a much more serious matter than simply a question of eating foods that are unhealthy.

Temptation, at its root, is about whether or not I, and we, will choose to live under God's loving rule. Temptation always offers us a choice – we can choose to live by God's wonderful loving ways or we can decide to go along with the majority. We can choose to live for God, or for ourselves.

But temptation is also an opportunity to grow. The Greek word most commonly used in the New Testament for 'temptation' can be equally well translated 'testing'. This is testing not in the sense of a school exam but rather in the sense of 'proving' – even 'improving'. In ancient times metal was heated so that the impurities could be removed and a purer metal formed; in this sense the metal was 'tested'. The events that happen in our lives which lead us to have to choose between God's word and way and our own act as opportunities for the fire of God's love to work within us. This 'holy fire' burns up the impurities and improves us in God's likeness, which is our holiness.

Temptation, further, is common to us all. I find it terribly easy to think, 'No one else finds their mind assaulted like I do.' I can look at someone whom I admire for their Christian faith and character and easily find myself thinking, 'It seems strange how little they seem to be tempted.' In both cases my thinking is false. Temptation is a totally common experience. As Paul wrote to the Christians in Corinth, 'No testing has overtaken you that is not common to everyone' (1 Corinthians 10.13).

So you face temptation to rage and anger, so do others; you face temptation to sexual infidelity, so do others; you face temptation to leave God out, so do others; you face the temptation of greed, so do others; you face the temptation to give up, so do others. In all these cases I need to say, 'And so do I.' We really are in this business of temptation and testing together; together with human beings across all cultures, and down through the ages. The temptations that I face are also faced by my friends in Rwanda, Australia, Brazil and Iran. The temptations you face were faced by people in the last century, and the one before that, and in the centuries of Abraham, Moses, David and Paul.

Furthermore we have a remarkable companion in all of our temptations. Jesus of Nazareth, according to the writer of the letter to the Hebrews, was like his brothers and sisters 'in every respect' (Hebrews 4.15). Jesus was not immune from human temptation; indeed rather the opposite. Again the writer to the Hebrews says this, 'Because he himself was tested by what he suffered, he is able to help those who are being tested,' and, 'For we do not have a high priest who is unable to sympathize with our weaknesses, but we have one who in every respect has been tested as we are, yet without sin' (Hebrews 2.18; 4.15).

This book seeks to take very seriously the reality of the temptations which face us. Together we will examine a range of the temptations that come our way. We will seek to understand them better and to see how, as tests, they can be growing points as well as pitfalls. Our travelling companion will be Jesus Christ himself. We will look at his life and ministry (the whole of it, not simply the most obvious stories of Jesus being tempted) to discover how it is that he was tempted like us and so is still able to help us. It is my simple prayer that as we are honest about the temptations with which we wrestle (and we must be honest about them if we are both to overcome them and grow through them), we will truly discover that they are opportunities to experience more of God's helping power. As we learn how to face temptation so we will find that these are tests through which we can grow more into the likeness of Jesus himself.

Ideas for reflection

1 Consider examples of advertising. (It may be helpful to have some magazines around, or watch a few adverts on commercial TV.) In what ways do these 'tempt' people?
2 Reflect on a personal experience of knowing what is the right thing to do, but choosing not to do it. Why did this happen? What could you have done differently?
3 Reflect on a personal experience when you knew you were tempted to act selfishly but chose not to do so. What helped you make this positive choice?

Picture

Jesus Mafa: *The Temptation of Jesus*

Prayer

Lord God, I come to you as one who is tempted in all kinds of ways.
Help me to learn how my temptations might prove to test me so that I am refined in your holy fire.
I pray in the name of the one who was tested in every way as I am,
Jesus Christ the Lord. Amen.

2

It happened to him too

It is simple to write that Jesus of Nazareth was 'tempted in every way as we are'. But what does it actually mean? In what ways was the carpenter who became a wandering preacher, teacher and healer tempted? How did he handle the temptations? In what ways did these temptations prove to be testing points for Jesus? Then, as we consider him, how can we learn from him so that we are better equipped ourselves to handle the temptations which come our way?

The writer to the Hebrews gives us a very clear description of the complete humanity of Jesus:

> Since, therefore, the children share flesh and blood, he himself likewise shared the same things, so that through death he might destroy the one who has the power of death, that is, the devil, and free those who all their lives were held in slavery by the fear of death. For it is clear that he did not come to help angels, but the descendants of Abraham. Therefore he had to become like his brothers and sisters in every respect, so that he might be a merciful and faithful high priest in the service of God, to make a sacrifice of atonement for the sins of the people. Because he himself was tested by what he suffered, he is able to help those who are being tested.
>
> (Hebrews 2.14–18)

Jesus shared the same human flesh as you and me. He was in no way shielded from the reality of living in this frail body. As a boy, an adolescent and a man, then, he experienced human life in all its joy, and all its anguish. Quite specifically, the writer tells us, he experienced temptation, testing, just as we do.

In case his readers had not quite got hold of this truth the writer reiterates it a little later: 'For we do not have a high priest who is unable to sympathize with our weaknesses, but we have one who in every respect has been tested as we are, yet without sin' (Hebrews 4.15).

Jesus, we are told, knows about human weaknesses. He knows about frailty, sadness and suffering. He knows about temptation for he has 'in every respect' been tested as we are. This statement comes as a real shock to many of Jesus' followers who somehow have managed to put him on a pedestal which removed him from some of the harsh realities of life. Some seem to think that when he cut himself Jesus did not bleed quite like the rest of us, or that when he miscued with a hammer his thumb did not bruise and there was no pain. But he did bleed, and there was pain and bruising. Some have the notion that when he was tired and weary he did not have the temptation to speak unkindly to one of the disciples. But he did face that temptation. He was tempted as we are 'in every respect'.

Now we need to explore this a little more closely. These words cannot mean 'in every exact same setting'. The writer to the Hebrews knew that himself. Jesus was never a tax collector, like Matthew; nor a woman like Mary Magdalene. Clearly, for example crossing the centuries, Jesus never sat in front of a computer which had yet again done something quite inexplicable and therefore wished to pick it up and destroy it by throwing it out of the window. Jesus, in his humanity, was a man not a woman. He cannot, therefore, have experienced the pains and agony of childbirth during which some women find themselves wanting to call the father of the child every rude name under the sun. Jesus died at the young age of 33. He cannot therefore have experienced within himself the specific temptations which come with old age. But what 'in every respect' does mean is that 'in every kind of way' that temptation and testing comes Jesus has experienced it. There is a generic nature to temptation and testing which shows itself in a thousand and one specific ways. Jesus cannot have experienced every specific one because of the limitations of living at a particular point of history, in a particular culture; as a Jewish male, dying young. But as a complete human being Jesus did experience every generic type of temptation and testing known to humankind. It is in this way, therefore, that he is able to understand us, and help us, as we face the same temptations as he did. As the commentator William Lane puts it,

> The emphatic statement that he was 'tested in every respect, in quite the same way we are' implies that he (Jesus) was susceptible to all the temptations that are connected with the weaknesses inherent in the frailty of humanity.
>
> (William L. Lane, *Word Biblical Commentary: Hebrews 1–8*)

The writer to the Hebrews does, however, state that there is one crucial point of difference between Jesus and the rest of humanity – he never gave in to temptation. He never sinned. I do. You do.

Two distinct difficulties arise for different groups of people at this point. For some the difficulty is that they find this impossible to believe; Jesus was a very good man, certainly; even the most perfect human who has ever lived, but sinless? For some this seems a step too far.

When the enemies of Jesus became determined to have him killed they sought every possible avenue to find something against him. Try as they might they could find nothing; not a hint of scandal or falsehood. Pontius Pilate had no reason to support Jesus, and yet he declared that he could find nothing wrong with Jesus. Now certainly Jesus' enemies and Pilate were looking for crimes worthy of serious punishment at this point. But for three years his enemies had been trying to find fault, any fault. Jesus' disciples lived as close to him as was possible for those three years, and yet they decided that no falsehood ever came from his lips.

Everything about him spoke of perfection and holiness. Somehow they could conclude that he was 'without sin'. As we shall see later when we look at Jesus' baptism, it was also the declaration of God himself on Jesus' life. So, hard though it may be to imagine, I find myself having to stand with the testimony of those who heard, saw with their own eyes, looked at and touched with their own hands (see 1 John 1.1) that Jesus of Nazareth, alone of all human beings, was without sin. But if you find it a step too far, hold on to Jesus as the finest example of humanity who has ever walked the earth and see how he handled temptation. Learn from him, even if 'sinless' is just too much to handle at present.

For others the difficulty is rather different. They accept Jesus as sinless but this therefore puts Jesus at a distance from them. He is therefore unable to help – he was perfect, I am not, so how can he help? In fact the complete opposite is the case. Jesus' experience of temptation was actually even greater than mine or yours, for as Philip Hughes puts it, 'Christ knows the full force of temptation in a manner that we who have not withstood it to the end cannot know it.'

Rather than his perfection distancing him from us, it draws us closer. Here is the one who offers us the way of handling temptation. Here is the one who offers us hope of overcoming. If as a fully fledged human being living in the power of the Spirit under the Father's love he could overcome temptation, he offers the possibility that we too might overcome; if not always, certainly sometimes. His life becomes our hope for living with temptation.

This leads to what, for me, is the most crucial lesson to learn from Jesus' experience of temptation. It is this. There is nothing wrong in experiencing temptation. Temptation is part of human experience.

This is vitally important to grasp as so often people fall into the trap of thinking that because they are tempted there is something wrong with their Christian discipleship. Arguably the very opposite is the truth. Temptation is a sign of being human and of being a disciple. Temptation is an opportunity for growth, not a sign of failure or defeat. As we grow in likeness to Jesus we are actually going to face greater and deeper temptations than we have previously done. Growing in Christlikeness does not remove us from temptation; it rather takes us deeper into it.

So, having set this background, as we move to reflect on our temptations and Jesus' actual experience of temptation, what we will be looking for is the generic nature of the temptations. What is at the heart of Jesus' experience of temptation? If we can discover this then we will be equipped to understand the heart of our own temptations. We will be looking to see how Jesus overcame the temptations – what, for him, were the 'ways of escape'. For if we can learn this from him who experienced deeper and harder temptations than we ever will do then we will be discovering how we might escape, overcome and become more like Christ through our testing.

We will not always succeed. Often we will fail. We will give in to our temptations. We will fail the tests. When this happens we will need to come back to him to 'receive mercy and find grace to help in time of need' (Hebrews 4.16). We will have to confess our failure and discover afresh the wonderful forgiving grace of God. But there will be times when, with the help of the Holy Spirit, we will overcome temptation. We will 'pass the test'. When we do so we will not become perfect but we will grow in our likeness to Jesus. Something more of his character and greatness will be marked in us, and so our lives will bring more glory to him.

Ideas for reflection

1 Meditate on the words of Hebrews 2.14–18 and 4.15–16.
2 What encourages you about Jesus being fully human and tempted in every way as we are?
3 What do you find difficult in thinking about Jesus being like us in temptation?
4 Boldly come to the throne of God's grace and ask for mercy and grace to help in time of need.

Picture

Jesus Mafa: *Jesus in Nazareth as a Child*

Prayer

Almighty God, whose Son Jesus Christ fasted forty days in the wilderness, and was tempted as we are, yet without sin: give us grace to discipline ourselves in obedience to your Spirit; and as you know our weakness, so may we know your power to save; through Jesus Christ our Lord, who is alive and reigns with you, in the unity of the Holy Spirit, one God, now and for ever. Amen.

(Collect for the First Sunday of Lent,
Common Worship)

3

It happens all the time

———◆◆◆———

Ever since I first heard of the 'Desert Fathers' I have found myself
rather mystified by them. These were men (there were also some
women but sadly, as has been the case throughout Christian
history, our records of them are rather sparse) who spent long
periods of time living alone in caves, or up mountains in the
heart of the Middle-Eastern deserts during the third, fourth and
fifth centuries. Some of them have enriched our lives ever since
through their writings and reflections. In their own day, people
would travel for days to go and speak with them. But God has
made us to be social creatures. We are not made to live in isolation, separate from the rest of the world. We are designed to live
in community. So the notion of going off deep into the desert
to live entirely alone for long periods has always seemed to me
somewhat contrary to how God has made us. If I'm being really
honest at times I think I have seen them as escapist; trying to run
away from the stark realities of life, and of community. Now I
remain mystified by them. However, as I have learned more about
them over the years I have come to understand that I had largely
misunderstood them. They were part of wider communities;
monastic communities living in isolated places certainly but
communities nevertheless. Their times in isolation were part of their
overall community life. This I can understand. I need time and
space alone and away from others myself. Being an introvert by
nature I gain strength from being alone; being with others can be
very draining for me – whereas for an extrovert this will usually
be invigorating and energizing.

However, my biggest change in understanding has come from the Desert Fathers' own description and recognition that being alone in the desert has not removed them from life at all. For in the desert they find themselves alone with their own inner thoughts, feelings and temptations – their own inner demons. Removal from the community, and indeed from all the basics of life, they universally declare, is not removal from temptation. If anything it brings a heightening of temptation. As George Lings notes when writing about the importance of being 'Alone' for members of the modern-day Northumbria Community,

> In Northumbria Community there is conscious dependence on the Desert tradition and a well-used phrase is 'your cell will teach you everything' . . . The (monastic) cell may be what we most flee from, for it will strip us of pretence, our glib second-hand opinions, and our preference for other experts to top up our spiritual bank balance and **most dreadfully it will show us ourselves**. But this is the doorway to truer liberation in Christ. As such, the desert is no place of escapism but rather of a stark reality. The cell is the address for finding our own vulnerability and being vulnerable to God.
>
> (*Encounters on the Edge No. 29*, Northumbria
> Community. George Lings, 2006)

As this book unfolds we will be examining some specific types of temptation that are faced by us all. At this point, though, I want simply to state that, just like you, the rest of humanity and Jesus himself, I am faced with temptation on a very regular basis. Indeed there is a daily struggle with one temptation or another. Whether I am at my desk, out and about visiting community and church leaders, with my family at home or with friends, temptation keeps appearing. Whether it is early in the morning, the middle of the day or I awake in the middle of the night, temptation can suddenly leap out at me. If I am in the wonders of the monkey-filled Nyungwe Forest (Rwanda) or the gentle beauty of the pony-filled New Forest (UK); if I am listening to music, reading or watching the TV, temptation of one kind or another can creep in around the corner. There is no clear rhyme or reason to when, where, how or in what way temptation may come but come it most certainly does. It has not lessened at all as I have grown older. It certainly has not lessened with the greater load of leadership to which God has called me over the years. Temptation simply is part of life, and will remain so until the day I die.

This having been said I would want to add that there have been periods of my life in which the temptations seem to have come more strongly for a time. These have often been associated with two factors.

Factor One. Times of particular spiritual blessing, whether personal or corporate, have regularly, at least it appears to me, been followed by particularly tough times of testing (again both personal and corporate). When I was regularly leading 'mission' weeks for churches, the week or two following were often filled with difficulties and traumas. After I have preached, encouraging the discipleship of others, I am regularly assailed by personal doubts and feelings of failure. The last thing I need immediately after preaching is criticism as I will usually be only too aware of my failings and frailties; what I need at that point is encouragement. Helpful criticism will be much more readily accepted a day or two later.

Factor Two. Times of stress, tiredness and weakness have often been compounded by the most severe of temptations. So when life seems to be almost at breaking point, then it is that a fresh temptation comes. This is usually a temptation either to escape, find an easy or quick way out or to give up and break. I am not one given to drinking alcohol a great deal, though I do enjoy a glass of red wine or a good pint of bitter, but the thought in times of great stress of having two or three too many drinks just to escape from it all has a great appeal. I am also amazed following my trips to Africa and experiencing intense poverty how strong the urge is to 'splash out' on some needless item of excess in the airport duty-free shop.

Sometimes the temptation to escape or give up is much more drastic than these two examples suggest. You may already have additionally noticed that Factor Two can readily occur following Factor One. After a spiritual 'high' we hit a 'low' and while in that 'low' further temptation arises. There is here a potential for a spiral of temptation. Perhaps particularly in these times I need to be reminded again that there is nothing wrong with temptation; it is an experience common to us all. It is giving in to it and falling into rebelling against God that is sin.

Throughout this book I share stories from my own life, and from those I have known. Quite deliberately there are stories from different points of my life. Stories from childhood, teenage years, and throughout my adult life; some of the stories are very recent events. This is because temptation has been a lifelong experience. It has changed shape through the years but it has been an ever-present reality. The truth is temptation happens to us all the time.

From where does temptation come?

Traditionally temptation has been regarded as coming from three sources, 'the world, the flesh and the devil'. By 'the world' is meant not the physical earth, but the system of the human community in its opposition to God and his rule. As John writes,

> For all that is in the world – the desire of the flesh, the desire of the eyes, the pride in riches – comes not from the Father but from the world. And the world and its desire are passing away, but those who do the will of God live for ever.
>
> (1 John 2.16–17)

Again John writes, 'We know that we are God's children, and that the whole world lies under the power of the evil one' (1 John 5.19). So temptation is seen as coming from outside of us through the community and society in which we are set. As we walk around the shops; as we watch our televisions with programmes proclaiming all kinds of morality; as we sit in the cinema; as we read or listen to music; when we are out clubbing with friends, or having a quiet drink in the pub; at our sports club or in the gym 'the world' with its different ways of thinking and priorities which are not focussed on God's glory continually seeks to tempt us into conformity with itself rather than into God's transforming ways.

Temptation is also seen as coming from the evil one, the devil, Satan; God's great adversary who is out to destroy God's purposes and usurp God's place. We will return to consider Satan a little later; for now we simply note him as the Tempter, and as the accuser of God's children.

The third source of temptation is seen as coming from within us, our own flesh. This is clearly taught by Jesus himself when he declared,

> It is what comes out of a person that defiles. For it is from within, from the human heart, that evil intentions come: fornication, theft, murder, adultery, avarice, wickedness, deceit, licentiousness, envy, slander, pride, folly. All these evil things come from within, and they defile a person.
>
> (Mark 7.20–23)

Paul expresses his own inner battling like this:

> But I am of the flesh, sold into slavery under sin. I do not understand my own actions. For I do not do what I want, but I do the very thing I hate . . . For I do not do the good I want, but the evil I do not want is what I do . . .
>
> (Romans 7.14–20)

My own experience bears all this out. It is inner desires which pull me away from living God's way and towards doing things which I know are wrong. Actions and words which will hurt, damage and upset others; actions and words which will not bring more good into the world; actions and words which will also damage me as a person, further marring God's image within me, pulling me away from the holy God. I am still horrified at the inner darkness which rises to the surface of my mind and my emotions at times;

the anger, violence, lust and destructiveness. I know that within me there lies the capacity for vile language, scorn, greed, hatred, murder, child abuse, adultery and every sin under the sun.

James' analysis I have always found very helpful. 'But one is tempted by one's own desire, being lured and enticed by it; then, when that desire has conceived, it gives birth to sin, and that sin, when it is fully grown, gives birth to death' (James 1.14–15). First there comes a selfish desire; if we recognize this we can cut it off at source. However, if we allow that desire to hang around in our minds and our emotions like an alluring finger beckoning us in, or a sweet-tongued word drawing us on, it starts enticing us towards itself. The desire becomes stronger and produces an idea, a way of fulfilment. This idea then gives birth to an action and that action is sin. At every point the move towards a sinful act can be stopped; at inception, and on the journey through. But it is easy to let the selfish desire rule and give birth to sinful words and deeds. I have discovered that recognizing all of this to be the truth, owning up to it before God, then seeking his power to overcome has been the source of not giving in to all such temptations. I cannot resist temptation by my own will alone; I need God's strength, and ways of escape.

Jesus – tempted all his life?

As Jesus came out of the waters of Jordan – following his baptism by John – Matthew, Mark and Luke all tell us that a voice came from heaven, saying, 'You are my Son, the Beloved; with you I am well pleased' (Luke 3.22).

Our tendency is to read these words and reflect on them for the time of the baptism and looking forward into the ministry which lies ahead. Certainly we are right to do so. But we should also reflect on what these words say to us about the first 30 years of Jesus' life. He has spent all these years, barring the very earliest days in Bethlehem and as a refugee in Egypt, living in Nazareth. He has grown up under the care and nurture of Mary and Joseph. He learned to sit, stand, walk and talk like every other child. He probably went to synagogue school, where he learned Hebrew, reading and writing and all about the Scriptures. He has played in the streets with the other children of the village. He has become a carpenter, and worked alongside his father within his local community and region. He has experienced life with his brothers, James, Joseph, Simon and Judas, and at least two, though probably more, sisters (Matthew 13.55f.). Probably he has experienced the death of his father, Joseph, and consequently had to take on the role of being male head of the household. He has experienced life in a mixed community, with Roman soldiers being commonplace. He has lived through the Roman mass crucifixion in Sepphoris just a few miles away (*c.*15 AD). He has experienced the ups and downs of good and bad harvests affecting everyone's lives. He knows all about the role of the scribes, the Pharisees and the tax collectors in the local community.

Now he has taken the enormous step of leaving home and family, travelling down to find his cousin John and deciding to undergo baptism – against his cousin's initial wish. It is this man upon whom, like a dove, the Holy Spirit descends and alights and whom God the Father addresses as 'my Son, the Beloved; with whom I am well pleased'.

This then is a statement of satisfaction and pleasure not simply referring to this act of baptism but a statement about all that has gone before. The whole 30 years that have passed, in all their apparent ordinariness of life, are well pleasing to God. Jesus could not now be embarking on his public ministry and mission with the Father's approval if all that had gone before had not also been approved by the Father. Jesus does not suddenly arrive at being the Son. He does not leap into this ministry. He has been preparing for it all of the time. Every lesson in synagogue school, every nail hammered in the workshop; every Sabbath worship; every meal time with the family; every engagement with his neighbours in the community of Nazareth has been part of this preparation – and upon it, in its entirety, the Father declares his pleasure. Now this must therefore teach us something about temptation and testing through the years of growing up and in ordinary everyday life – for if Jesus has been tempted in every respect as we are then he has experienced this in growing up and in ordinary life. A few moments' reflection should help us here.

We are given little direct information about Jesus' childhood in the Gospels. But the small amount we are given in Luke offers us considerable insight: 'The child grew and became strong, filled with wisdom; and the favour of God was upon him' (Luke 2.40). This verse at least tells us that as Jesus grew up he had to learn, and in particular he had to learn to make choices. He proved to be one who was able to make wise choices – for he was filled with wisdom. Such was this wisdom throughout these earliest years that it was recognized that 'God's favour was on him'. He was not a child protégé, or a child miracle worker but there was in his approach to life at five, and at every age, a wisdom which showed. Then at the age of 12 he makes the journey to Jerusalem for the Passover festival as part of the whole local community. His parents leave Jerusalem contentedly thinking that Jesus is with other family members. But at the end of the day when he does not reappear they become worried and return to Jerusalem, concluding that this is where he must be. They are right but it takes them time to find him. In this story we then have to note the depth of Jesus' own self-consciousness about his responsibility: 'I must be in my Father's house' (Luke 2.49).

His understanding of his relationship with the Father is developing and maturing. It is not in a place yet ready for all that will happen once he is 30 but it is growing. But then Luke notes, 'Then he went down with them and came to Nazareth, and was obedient to them . . . And Jesus increased in wisdom and in years, and in divine and human favour' (Luke 2.51–52).

There is a temptation here for Jesus to move ahead sooner than his Father wants. There is at least an indication of childhood/ adolescent impatience which he brings under control. There is a clear statement that Jesus recognizes the rightness of remaining under his parents' responsibility. Any temptation to move out of this he resists. Luke reflects further on the developing wisdom – the ability to make the right choices and decisions at the right moment. He also notes a growth in human favour. In other words there is in Jesus a social development. In this there must have been the possibility of making unhelpful relationships; of creating social barriers and the like. But apparently Jesus avoids these. He simply keeps growing in favour with God and people.

Now with all due reverence let me remind you that Jesus' growth in human stature through these years meant that he went through puberty. He experienced discovering hairs in places where there were none before. He experienced all the bodily changes associated with human growth and development. So he faced the same temptations that face every teenage male. He was in an age and a culture which approached all of this very differently from our own but he still experienced it all. Yet he did so without ever falling short of the Father's holy standards. As he went into early adulthood he doubtless faced questions about when he would marry – and questions about why he did not do so.

In the world of his work there would have been those around who would happily take short cuts; overcharge and cheat. Bribery and corruption were well known in the Roman world and would have impacted business in Galilee. There were those who were so appalled at the Roman regime that they determined to defeat them through violence, and what today we call terrorist acts. The Zealots were active and might have tried recruiting the carpenter. In the world of faith there were plenty who were willing to compromise on the demands of the Law, as well as those who sought to make the Law ever more demanding. Jesus saw and heard it all – that becomes very clear when his public ministry gets under way. But he continually through these years chose to simply stay faithful to the way of the Scriptures.

Then what about his own calling? It seems clear from Mary's conversation with him at the wedding of Cana that at least from time to time the two of them had discussions about his calling and work – she has an anticipation and expectation about him which leads her to intervene in this wedding scene. His cousin John has been growing in popularity and pointing ahead to the coming of the Messiah. How often did Jesus, I wonder, contemplate leaving the family home before he finally made that decisive step? What held him at home? I think most probably his responsibilities as son and older brother. Fulfilling his Father's will included ensuring the family were properly cared for until they were in a position to do so for themselves – but then the time comes to leave.

You see Jesus knows what living ordinary life is all about. He understands what it is to hold down a job, live in a family, be part of a local community. He experienced the temptations and tests that come with the simple ordinariness of everyday living. So he is able to help us handle the very same temptations and tests. We are not alone, we can come to him, boldly, and seek mercy when we fail, and grace to help us in our need so that we can stand up in the face of our everyday temptations.

Throughout this book we will find ourselves examining Jesus' temptations through the rest of his life; his three years of public ministry. These temptations were stronger than anything I have ever faced. This leads me to understand that Jesus knew within himself the temptation to all kinds of evil. Yet he never allowed that desire to give birth to sin – that is the key difference between him and everyone else who has ever lived. He knew the temptations of the flesh, as well as those of the world and the devil, but he never sinned. Because he knew them he is able to understand us; because he resisted them he is able to help us; because he overcame them he is able to offer us forgiveness.

So what about the devil?

If so much temptation comes from our own inner desires, and from the world around us, where do the devil and demons fit in?

One answer is to regard the devil and demons as an ancient idea whose time has passed. I confess this has its attractions. Certainly much of what may well have been put down to Satan and demons in times past we now understand in either physical or psychological terms. However, to simply interpret all references to the devil and the demonic in this way seems to me to lack a degree of faithfulness to Scripture, and also to fail to take seriously the experience of people around the world today.

In regard to taking Scripture seriously it is the experience and approach of Jesus which is paramount. Mark offers us a very brief account of Jesus' temptations in the wilderness. 'And the Spirit immediately drove him out into the wilderness. He was in the wilderness for forty days, tempted by Satan' (Mark 1.12–13). Mark here depicts the 40 days as a direct conflict with Satan. This introduces a theme which runs throughout Mark's Gospel. Jesus' ministry will frequently be seen as a conflict with the powers of darkness that hold humans captive. Jesus comes to defeat evil, cast out the evil powers and bring release to those held captive. Now for many of us the notion of Satan is a difficult one. Our problem, I would like to suggest, is that our image of Satan is drawn more from Dante's *Inferno*, Christopher Marlowe's *Faustus*, John Milton's *Paradise Lost* and the enduringly popular image of the red, two-horned, fork-tailed, spear-carrying devil, rather than from the Scriptures' own words. The Bible's image, which develops somewhat hazily through its pages, is of the malevolent one who seeks to disrupt God's purposes. In Jesus' own later description the devil is a 'liar and the father of lies' and a 'murderer' (John 8.44). He is also Beelzebul (Mark 3.22–30). In the words of Revelation he is 'the accuser' (Revelation 12.10), which is what strictly the name Satan means. Here in the story of the temptation his existence and reality as one determined to disrupt and destroy God's work is clear. I have to say that I find a lot of writing and theology about Satan and the demonic quite fanciful (for example the often entertaining, but theologically problematic, novels of Frank Peretti). But the witness of the Scriptures is clear enough that there exist real evil, demonic forces and that the devil is not to be dismissed as legend but rather is a reality.

I find this further enhanced by Paul's description of the Church's spiritual warfare being with 'principalities and powers' (Ephesians 6.12; Colossians 2.15). Walter Wink's writings have been enormously helpful in showing how these describe not so much tiny little demons hiding under our beds but rather sweeping forces which pervade and create social and political constructs which seek to place humanity, or economics, or an ideology above the one and only true God.

If then we take the existence of Satan as a reality, in line with Jesus himself, then we also need to note his limits. Satan must be a created being, therefore strictly limited. Satan was bound to attack the Son of God but is unlikely to worry too much about most of us ordinary believers. Certainly demonic forces, under Satan's rule, will work to destroy people and communities. I have seen and heard enough evidence in this country and in other parts of the world to know that a person can be taken over by strong inhuman forces; and that in Jesus' name those same people can find freedom and release. I have also seen how malevolent destructive forces can create havoc within a church community as well as within the wider community. But I fear that far too often we use the existence of the demonic to deflect blame. 'It wasn't me; I was tempted to do it.' 'Don't blame me; it's the devil's fault.' Such words have been used from the beginning of humanity to try and shift the blame for our own sin and failure on to someone or something else.

So yes, there is a real being Satan; yes, the demonic realm exists but we must never use its existence as a way of deflecting the blame for our own human frailty and our own decision to give in to temptation – whether it comes from within us, or from outside of us.

Mark's temptation account takes us further. It is clear that Jesus is seen here as defeating and overcoming Satan in this time in the wilderness. It does not mean this is the end of such a battle for Jesus – the rest of the Gospel will make it quite clear that the conflict is not over – but Jesus is the Victorious One. This victory will be worked out through the cross. In Jesus we discover the

Overcomer, the Victorious One, the one who triumphs over Satan in every circumstance. So as we have been baptized into Christ, as through faith we have entered God's grace and been adopted into his family in Christ, we can be victorious over the evil one when he tempts us.

Daily temptation

So temptation will be a part of our lives until the day we die. It was for Jesus himself. Temptation will come to us from outside, through demonic powers, yes; through the world around us, certainly; from within us – most of the time. Temptation will sometimes hit us right between the eyes (on occasions quite literally). It will also creep up on us slowly from behind. It will whisper seductively in our ears. There will be occasions when it feels like temptation has our arm up hard against our back, or is like a gun being held to our head. Yet we must continually remind ourselves that temptation in itself is not wrong; it is part of our human experience. Jesus himself faced it – and with a force and ferocity that we will never know.

Jesus overcame temptation. He offers us his companionship, through the Holy Spirit, to help us overcome ourselves. When we fail he offers us his forgiveness and a fresh start in the daily fight.

Ideas for reflection

1 How helpful do you find the description of temptation coming from 'the world, the flesh and the devil'?
2 Recall a personal experience of a spiritual 'high' being followed by a time of temptation. What was it? How did it feel? What helped you through such a time?
3 Take time to reread Mark 1.12–13. What are your wilderness experiences like?
4 What for you is the value of being 'alone'? What are the difficulties?

5 Why not plan a day alone with God – find a retreat house, or go on a long walk, or find a quiet beach. Take nothing but yourself, a Bible, a notebook and food and drink (no alcohol) for the day. Keep a journal of what God reveals to you about yourself through the day.

Pictures

Jesus Mafa: *Temptation in the Wilderness*
Sidney Spencer: *Driven by the Spirit into the Wilderness*

Prayer

Father, temptations come to me from the world around, from the evil one and from within. Give me the wisdom to recognize temptations for what they are; give me the insight to choose your way, and give me the strength of your Spirit to live for the good. I pray in the name of the one who overcame, Jesus Christ the Lord. Amen.

4

Falsehood and truth

The opening story in the book was a public confession of my own capacity for lying and deception. Sadly I could recount many examples from my own life. I do not make a habit of lying. I seek to be truthful. But I would have to confess to resorting to lying for a whole host of reasons.

I can think back to my school days and remember lying about homework that was never completed. The teacher, I suspect now not really believing me, accepted the lie that I had spilt a flower vase of water all over it just before leaving home. Or again, when wanting an excuse to miss school for a day, eating some soap to make me feel sick and persuade my mum that I really was too ill to go to school that day. These might now seem relatively trivial through adult eyes. At the time, however, they felt serious, and in their own way they were. They involved deceit of parents and teachers. Lying, when discovered, inevitably leads to an undermining of truth and trust.

Throughout my adulthood I have sought to cover my tracks on occasions by lying. 'I'm sorry; it hasn't arrived yet. The Post Office seems to become more and more unreliable, doesn't it? I'll send you a copy.' Then the letter is written and sent. 'It's the next on the list of things to do', when actually it has been forgotten or even deliberately pushed to one side hoping that it will go away.

Such outright lying, I hope you'll be pleased to read, is a rare event (even very rare? Or am I deluding myself now?) in my life. But I am conscious of how easy it is to slide into the use of half-truth, or at least colouring an event or story to ensure that I come out of it in the better, or even best, light.

In the early months of my time in Walthamstow we had an all-age event in our church school. It had been a great deal of fun and very successful. There was only one problem; no one seemed to want to go home and some of the children had become overexcited and exuberant. I was very tired and was becoming increasingly frazzled. 'I've got to get everyone out quickly,' I thought to myself. I stood on a block and bellowed over everyone. 'Stop everyone. There's a fire in the corner. No need to panic but we must have everyone out of the room immediately.'

Everyone did stop. The room emptied quickly and apparently without alarm. There were only two problems; there was no fire, and outside there were some quite scared young children. It was an extremely stupid thing to do. The anger that came in my direction over the next few hours, and days, was sometimes over the top but certainly not unfounded. The trouble was that I compounded it all by stubbornly refusing to admit how stupid I had been for some hours. I tried to defend myself and deflect the anger elsewhere, even to subtly try and persuade angered parents that it was really their own fault for failing to properly control their own children. To this day I shiver slightly at the memory of my own stupidity in using that lie. On that occasion the lying openly landed me in deep trouble; on others it may seem to have protected me. But it has never protected me from myself or from the all-seeing ears and eyes of God himself.

I have recounted personal stories. The sad truth is that we see and hear lies across our society each and every day of our lives. I have a deep respect for local and national politicians who work extremely hard for the good of local communities and the nation. They are often harshly and unfairly treated and criticized. However, they do not help themselves when they are 'economical with the truth' by overtly lying, giving only half the story or deliberately trying to rubbish their opponents. Sadly this happens far too much in our local and national political life.

Newspaper, radio and TV journalists can also fall foul of the truth for the sake of producing sales, listening or viewing figures. Photographs of celebrities are 'doctored' so that a rumour can be started about an affair which has no basis in reality. Stories can be published which have rather less than a shred of truth within them – and when they are exposed all we get is a tiny three-line correction hidden away in the depths of the paper or as a late-night apology between programmes noting that a complaint has been upheld.

TV soap opera storylines live by the constant use of telling lies, half-truths or simply a failure to speak the truth. How often I wonder have I sat wanting to shout at a soap character, 'Just tell the truth'? But they don't.

In offices, factories, classrooms, staff rooms, rest homes, community centres, sports clubs, churches, and above all in homes, up and down the land we all so easily give in to the temptation to choose to lie, or embellish the facts, rather than speak the truth. For some it becomes completely habit-forming, and truth-telling seems to become the exception rather than the rule.

Closely associated with this is the power and destructiveness of gossip. Gossip fills the pages of magazines and newspapers; it meanders around the office corridors; it can dominate the life of clubs, societies and community centres. When I was a curate, in Wandsworth, I loved dropping in at the local community centre for a coffee and a chat with the staff and members of the local community. It was often great fun and lots of laughter happened. The people there were 'the salt of the earth'. However, the whole life of the centre came to a serious crisis because of the gossip put around by a few people about two others who were regularly there. The gossip was vicious and malicious. It was driven by jealousy. Somehow I, along with one or two key local community members, managed to help most people see that it was all untrue. We lost friendship with the perpetrators of the gossip who would not back down and decided to absent themselves from the centre. But the life of the centre as a whole was rescued through the truth being revealed.

I have known people who have suffered greatly from gossip being circulated about them. It is hard to counteract sometimes. You will hear people saying, 'There's no smoke without fire', implying that for gossip to exist there must be some truth in the story. On occasions that is so, but I have certainly known times where there was no truth in the gossip whatsoever and it caused immense pain and damage. The only way to defeat gossip is to confront it with the truth. Sadly gossip has always infected church life (see 2 Corinthians 12.20; 1 Timothy 5.13; 3 John 10) as well as wider society (Romans 1.29). I have no hesitation in saying that I believe it is just as serious an issue for church life as questions of abuse of power, financial probity and sexual morality, but often not tackled as seriously as these.

Lying, deceit and gossip create for all of us an ever-encircling trap of our own making. When we think we are in danger of being trapped by our own lies we easily deceive ourselves into thinking that we can escape through further lies rather than speaking the truth. The fresh lies only tighten the cord around our own necks, and too often around the necks of others involved as well. Lying, deceit and gossip put us into bondage. They make us captive to their own world of falsehood.

In complete contrast Jesus declared, 'The truth will make you free' (John 8.32). He had observed the power of lies over people's lives. The lies of the Pharisees who he had the courage to declare to be 'blind guides'; the lies of the Sadducees who failed to see any possibility of angelic life and ministry or of resurrection; and the lies of the priestly caste in Jerusalem.

Was Jesus ever tempted to lie, or to be economical with the truth? Certainly he was.

Jesus speaking the truth

Right at the outset of his public ministry we find a clear test for Jesus about speaking the truth. His public ministry started very successfully; Luke tells us that after his baptism by John the

Baptist, 'Jesus, filled with the power of the Spirit, returned to Galilee, and a report about him spread through all the surrounding country. He began to teach in their synagogues and was praised by everyone' (Luke 4.14–15). Then Jesus returns to his home town of Nazareth. Inevitably there would have been a different feel from Capernaum and the other villages. Here Jesus is surrounded by familiar faces. His elders, his own family, his contemporaries and his juniors are all here in his home synagogue. They are eager to listen to their home-grown prophet. There must have been some excitement and a real sense of anticipation. You can feel this as Luke recounts the story: 'the eyes of all in the synagogue were fixed on him' (Luke 4.20).

As Jesus looked around into their faces he had a decision to make. 'Do I speak the truth or do I hold back? Do I hold on to the favour I have with these friends and neighbours or do I risk losing it by explaining the word of the Lord?'

He chose the way of truth rather than popularity. He chose the costly path of humble obedience. Initially it creates an okay reaction (Luke 4.22). But then as he explains how God works for the outsider it begins to dawn on them that he is not going to be contained by them so they turn nasty. In fact they turn very nasty and threaten to throw him off a cliff to his death (Luke 4.28–29).

We will all face situations from time to time when we are called upon to speak the truth. It may be with a member of the family, or a neighbour, or a church member. It may be as a church leader in preaching or at a church leadership meeting. We know there is a truth that needs to be spoken, but we equally know that the response and reaction may not be favourable. At such times we have to learn the courage of resisting keeping people sweet and speaking the truth. There are ways of doing so which are gracious, thoughtful and loving rather than hectoring or overpowering, but learning to speak the truth in love is something we all need to do.

When on trial before the High Priest, Jesus was challenged as to whether or not he was the Christ; Jesus replies, 'Yes, it is as you say' (Matthew 26.64, NIV). He could have toned it down. It must have been tempting to do so because he knew what the honest reply would mean. He chose to speak the truth.

But Jesus was not always as blunt with the truth as when describing the Pharisees as blind guides, or acknowledging that he was the Messiah when on trial before the High Priest. He could be highly enigmatic at times. The whole use of parables was a means of communicating truth but in a way which said, 'Work this out for yourselves.' Many of the parables end with Jesus' words, 'Let anyone with ears listen!' (e.g. Matthew 13.9). Jesus himself explains that he teaches in parables so that the meaning is not clear, even hidden from some (Matthew 13.13–17).

When John the Baptist is, understandably, going through a period of questioning whether or not Jesus really was the one for whom he was the prophetic forerunner, Jesus gives an answer which at first reading can seem a little obscure. But when one recognizes the clear use by Jesus of prophetic words from Isaiah it becomes plain that he is saying 'Yes' but with bags of evidence – the miracles he is performing fulfil the trustworthy words of the Scriptures John loved and knew (Matthew 11.1–6 citing Isaiah 35.4–6; 61.1).

It seems Jesus made very conscious decisions throughout his life and ministry to speak the truth but to do so in a wide variety of ways depending on who he was speaking with at the time, the nature of the conversation and the setting. He chose to express the truth through story, quoting the Scriptures, drawing on examples from life (Luke 14.28–33), remaining silent (John 8.6), asking questions (John 8.10) and sometimes speaking very bluntly. He was always passionate about and for the truth, knowing that this is what sets us free. But how he expressed the truth varied enormously.

Passionate for truth

This then offers us a pattern for living by the truth today. We need to be, indeed must be, passionate for the truth – God's truth. So we have to put lying and deceit aside. As St Paul put it, 'Do not lie to one another, seeing that you have stripped off the old self with its practices' (Colossians 3.9) and 'So then, putting away false-hood, let all of us speak the truth to our neighbours' (Ephesians 4.25). We have to embrace speaking the truth.

At its very simplest this means learning to think before we speak. It means learning how to bite our tongue so that we stop telling the lie or the half-truth. It means refusing to indulge in passing on gossip. It means learning to listen carefully before jumping in with our own ideas. It means putting into practice the words of St James, 'Be quick to listen and slow to speak' (James 1.19) for as he later sharply warns us,

> the tongue is a small member, yet it boasts of great exploits. How great a forest is set ablaze by a small fire! And the tongue is a fire. The tongue is placed among our members as a world of iniquity; it stains the whole body, sets on fire the cycle of nature, and is itself set on fire by hell.
>
> (James 3.5–6)

But our choice is not simply to refrain from speaking to stop gossip spreading or to speak the truth bluntly on every occasion. Our choice is to determine how best to speak the truth in each setting with the people/person we are addressing at the time. Experience tells us that to be blunt is often counterproductive. Finding ways of helping people see the truth for themselves, through a story or an example, is often far more effective and productive. It can, equally, be even more dangerous. When the penny drops the exposed person may react strongly against us – just as the Pharisees did against Jesus when the truth of the parables hit home. But for the sake of freedom we need to be people of truth. Truth is best for individuals, for families, for communities and for nations. Truth is often painful at first but it leads us into freedom.

The temptation to hide the truth away through lying and deceit will come regularly. The temptation to make ourselves look better by lying or telling a 'white lie' will come our way time and again. The temptation to indulge in 'a harmless bit of gossip' will be frequent. We have to learn to recognize how dangerous giving in to falsehood actually is for ourselves, our communities, our nation and our world. We need to recover the power of the truth and enter into truth's freedom by learning to speak the truth in love.

Ideas for reflection

1 Have you ever been, or can you think of someone you know who has been, the victim of gossip? What were the consequences of this gossip? What might have been/was done to stop it?
2 Why does the truth sometimes come across better in a story than being spoken bluntly?
3 Are there any current situations at work/in the home/in the community/church where truth needs to bring freedom? What might you do about this?

Pictures

Jesus Mafa: *The Beatitudes*
Dinah Roe Kendall: *Jesus and Peter in the Courtyard*

Prayer

Lord, you are the truth. Forgive me for all the lies, half-truths and gossip in which I indulge. Teach me to stand for truth; to speak the truth and to discover that the truth sets me free. Amen.

5

Worry and trust

'I cannot go to sleep, David is not in yet. He's never this late back from his group.' It was 11.30 p.m. I was talking to my wife Rosemary. I started playing all kinds of scenarios through my mind; was he lying slumped over the wheel of the car unconscious? Or in Southampton's A&E department being resuscitated? Or was he simply still chatting with friends, oblivious of the time? It is extraordinary where the mind and emotions can run in a short space of time when worry and anxiety start to take hold. I tell myself not to be stupid, not to think the worst and calm down; but quite easily the anxiety kicks back in and the scenes play over again, or become even worse. Needless to say around midnight the front door opened and David could be heard climbing the stairs. I stepped on to the landing and greeted him, noting that he was rather late. Quite understandably, oblivious to all my anxiety, he simply said, 'Yes, goodnight.'

Worry and anxiety affect us all. Different people worry about different things. Some, for example, never seem too worried about money while for many this is the biggest concern of all. Some worry about health and fitness even though they appear to most of us to be among the healthiest and fittest people we know. Even within the same family and household the matters which cause individuals worry can vary a great deal; this is certainly the case in our household. Some of the differences certainly relate to our age and responsibilities; you will not be surprised to know that it is the parents, for example, who express the most anxiety about young people's driving, and about matters like pensions and household maintenance. Younger family members are more worried by their appearance, and acceptance by peers. Some who think they know me well are surprised when they discover the levels of worry and anxiety that afflict me. I worry every time I step up to lead worship, or preach. I worry that I will not communicate clearly; I worry about what people will hear and experience; I worry about what they will think of me; I worry about making mistakes, especially ones which might lead to embarrassment. I have certainly worried a great deal about how people will respond to this book! I manage to hide the worry from most of the people most of the time. Yet those who know me best do know that this is part of life for me.

Worry and anxiety are part of life for all of us. For some they are extremely serious and debilitating. Over the years I have known many people who suffer from serious panic or anxiety attacks. I have dealt pastorally with those who are 'inveterate worriers'. Worry almost seems to be the middle name of some people. Worry is so intense for some that it leads to serious medical conditions that require medication or counselling and support. Billions of pounds are spent every year in the health service on drugs that are prescribed because the level of anxiety has reached such a pitch that nerves need to be calmed, depression needs to be brought under control.

For this is the reality of worry; it can lead to fear and to depression. Agoraphobia (fear of the outside/open spaces), claustrophobia (fear of confined spaces), arachnophobia (fear of spiders) and many more phobias besides often begin with a simple anxiety which develops into full-blown fear.

My own anxiety in the story above shows a degree of fear; fear for David's safety; fear of the bad driving habits of others – not his own, he's a very good driver; fear, even, of losing him.

Now before plunging us all into overanxiety about our worries let's pause for a moment and consider when worry, anxiety and even fear might be helpful and positive.

Positive worry

The sun was shining gloriously on the golden Cornish sands; the sea was a fabulous blue and the waves were great for body-boarding and surfing. It was beautiful. We were with very good friends enjoying it all. Rupert had gone off in his wetsuit, body-board in hand, to the designated area for boarding. He was, after all, the serious body-boarder among us. We were based a little way along the beach, which was very full; the wave-filled sea crowded. Lots of people were swimming, body-boarding and surfing. Rupert's mum lost sight of him. The wind changed and the waves suddenly became larger and more powerful. She began to worry that he would fall off the board, bang his head and no one would notice. Some of this worry was totally reasonable and sane; it was also natural; a mother caring for her child. A healthy awareness of the power of the sea is important. Ask any sailor, whether of small dinghies or huge tankers, and they will tell you that it is vital never to lose a healthy respect for and even fear of the power of the sea.

A fireman once told me exactly the same about fire. 'It is essential,' he said, 'that I never lose respect for the power of fire; a healthy fear of its capacity to hurt is the key to staying safe.' The same could be said of wind, electricity, gas and so on. While my own feeling is that as a culture we have become risk-assessment crazy, a healthy and wise analysis of risk makes complete sense.

A degree of fear, or anxiety, helps us act thoughtfully, soberly and with a right judgement. But overanxiety, and allowing worry and fear to start dominating us, lead into illness, or a paralysis of action. Fear of open spaces leads to someone, in extreme cases, being paralysed from leaving their home. Following the horrendous terrorist attacks on London's Underground and buses in July 2005 (now known as 7/7) many have been left fearful of ever using a bus or tube again – even though the actual risk remains minimal. The now 'ever-present' risk of aerial terrorism leaves some unable to ever contemplate going on an aeroplane. Fear, for some, has taken control.

Are worries and fear temptations?

It was the school summer fair and for weeks beforehand the whole class had been practising a country dance. It involved a variety of skipping and movement around the playground. At various points we each ended up in a hoop on the ground. The perimeter was crowded with parents, grandparents and people from the local community. My parents were there. The music began and we all began to dance. Quite where it went wrong I could not tell you. I was only six at the time. But two of us found ourselves standing in the same hoop while one nearby remained empty. I pushed my classmate, gently, towards the other hoop; he pushed me back whispering that I was in the wrong place. Suddenly Mrs Collins, our teacher, appeared and pulled me across to the vacant hoop; 'This is your hoop, Paul.' I was mortified and very embarrassed. I felt I had been shown up in front of everybody. Afterwards some of my friends laughed at me for getting it wrong. I have no hesitation in stating now that it was that incident which to this day has left me worried about making a mistake in public, of being embarrassed in front of a crowd. It may seem daft and irrational but it is true. I tell the story to illustrate the fact that some of our worries and fears arise from events that take place in our lives, particularly in our early lives. These incidents can at the time to most seem insignificant and trivial, but to the person concerned can shape them for the rest of their lives. (This can be positive shaping as well, of course.)

But if my continued worries about public embarrassment find their root in that far-off incident, can we really think of such worries and fears as 'temptations'? I believe we can and should. Let us stick with this particular example for a little longer. When I am all dressed up in my bishop's finery in the cathedral I am in the public eye (at least I certainly feel that I am!). This is just the kind of occasion when my fear of embarrassment can take hold. Therefore I can usually be seen before the service carefully checking with the precentor (usually the one in charge of the service organization) the exact details of what is expected of me. During the service there will usually be more than one surreptitious look by myself at the instructions, just to make sure I have got it right. On one occasion when for some reason or other I was particularly anxious (probably because there were more dignitaries than ever present) I had such a huge sense of relief that we had safely reached the end that I completely forgot to escort the mayor out of the cathedral. The temptation for me in all of this is to allow the fear and anxiety to take over. This is a matter of my decision of the will. I can choose to allow the anxiety to rule, or I can decide, yes to be aware of it, but not let it take over.

When fears are particularly profound it is highly unlikely that a person can just stop them dominating. Small steps and decisions have to be made to overcome the fear step by step. Medication for anxiety is eased back rather than simply stopped. Yet in these situations too there is a decision of the will being made to resist the temptation to give in to the worry or the fear and to live differently.

Jesus and worry

The most frequent words God ever speaks to human beings in the Bible are 'Fear not' (or as we are more likely to put it today, 'Do not be afraid'). Abraham, Hagar, Moses, Joshua, Israel as a nation, Joseph, Mary, the disciples and Paul among others, all heard these words. Jesus would have known them well as he learned the Scriptures through his growing years; and as he heard his parents' own stories around his own conception and birth.

As he sets out into his public ministry the Father gives him the antidote to any sense of fear that he might have had: 'You are my Son, the Beloved; with you I am well pleased' (Mark 1.11). Jesus' security lay in knowing who he was, and being sure that he was loved.

Some of my anxieties arise from the longing to be liked, to be thought well of by others. I can become worried about being successful and achieving things. Yet the antidote to worry is not about being liked, nor about success and achievement. The antidote to worry is being secure in knowing that I am utterly loved by God himself.

In his teaching Jesus made these very clear and firm points about worry and anxiety:

> Therefore I tell you, do not worry about your life, what you will eat or what you will drink, or about your body, what you will wear. Is not life more than food, and the body more than clothing? Look at the birds of the air; they neither sow nor reap nor gather into barns, and yet your heavenly Father feeds them. Are you not of more value than they? And can any of you by worrying add a single hour to your span of life? And why do you worry about clothing? Consider the lilies of the field, how they grow; they neither toil nor spin, yet I tell you, even Solomon in all his glory was not clothed like one of these. But if God so clothes the grass of the field, which is alive today and tomorrow is thrown into the oven, will he not much more clothe you – you of little faith? Therefore do not worry, saying, 'What will we eat?' or 'What will we drink?' or 'What will we wear?' For it is the Gentiles who strive for all these things; and indeed your heavenly Father knows that you need all these things. But strive first for the kingdom of God and his righteousness, and all these things will be given to you as well. So do not worry about tomorrow, for tomorrow will bring worries of its own. Today's trouble is enough for today.
>
> (Matthew 6.25–34)

God is our loving, caring Father, says Jesus, and it is in that confidence that we can live. Worry resolves nothing. It creates a tendency either to overactivism, or to a resigned fatalism. Faith in God's loving care allows us to focus on the heart of life – seeking God's rule and justice in all things.

Jesus was tempted to worry; he was tempted in every way just as we are. Jesus was tempted to give in to fear. For example, he became exasperated with his disciples' lack of faith and insight following the feeding of the 5,000 and the 4,000 (Matthew 16.5–12).

Something similar happens again on his descent from the Mount of Transfiguration (Matthew 17.14–18). In Gethsemane the anguish over all that lies ahead of him must have created inner fears. He was tempted to call down legions of angels to come to his aid. But he trusted rather in his Father's will, and he held on to his conviction that his death would be for the salvation of all, and that on the third day he would be raised. Worry that he had got it wrong; fear of the public humiliation he would face, and the pain he would undergo could all have tempted him to stop. Instead he lived out his own teaching: 'Do not worry about tomorrow. Today's trouble is enough for today.'

My worries and fears may often have their roots in early, or even later, life experiences. Previous failures, or let-downs, stir up emotions and thoughts within me that lead to fresh anxiety. Or the anxieties may arise because of the unknown that lies before me; new experiences, new challenges; new people to meet; new tasks to face – all of these can create fear. The temptation, always, is to give in to that fear; to allow it to dominate and determine how I will act; to stop me from facing new challenges, attempting new things or developing new relationships.

Jesus' example shows me rather to trust; to live in the deep knowledge that I am known and loved by God above and beyond all my anxieties. This reality does not necessarily mean that the anxious thoughts and emotions disappear (they rarely do); it rather gives me the strength and the courage to move through them and beyond them. To step out in faith and discover God's loving presence and strength in new places and new ways. Fear holds me back; living in trust of God's love enables me to grow.

Ideas for reflection

1 Can you identify what things cause you most worry and anxiety?
2 Are there events in your life which have created some of these?
3 What ways have you found to overcome worry and fear and express trust in God's loving care?

4 Do you know someone whose life is seriously crippled by anxiety/fear? How could you help them?

Pictures

Jesus Mafa: *Martha and Mary*
Sidney Spencer: *Consider the Lilies*

Prayer

The LORD is my light and my salvation;
whom shall I fear?
The LORD is the stronghold of my life;
of whom shall I be afraid?
Teach me your way, O LORD,
and lead me on a level path.
Help me to wait for you,
to be strong,
and let my heart take courage in you. Amen.

(Based on Psalm 27.1, 11, 14)

6

Money and contentment

The phone rang. It was a very poor line but I could just make out Enoch's voice at the other end. We were due to collect him, and his wife Phoebe, from Gatwick airport just a few hours later. He had time simply to say that they had had to return to their home in Kabale but would be on the plane 24 hours later than expected. The line went dead. There had been no time for explanations and we were not yet in the age of the mobile phone. I had no way of calling him back. So all we could do was wonder, pray and, yes, worry. The fact that he was clear that they would still be arriving 24 hours later was the calming factor. Whatever the situation clearly it was not so serious that they needed to postpone for several days, or even cancel. So 24 hours later we were at Gatwick to collect them both. There was much joy, and relief, when they walked through the exit to greet us. As we travelled to our home in Wandsworth they told us the story.

They had left their youngest children in the care of their grandparents at their home in Kabale. While Enoch and Phoebe were still in the coach on its six-hour journey to Kampala the house had been burgled. Everything had been stolen. Now by 'everything' they meant all the mattresses on which they slept on the floor (no beds); all their plates (enough for one each); all their cutlery (again one set for each family member); their cooking pots and the jerry cans they used to collect the water every day from the reasonably nearby well. The few clothes that belonged to the children had remained; Enoch and Phoebe had all their own clothes in the rather small suitcases which were now in the boot of our car. They had had very little, but even the little that they had owned was gone. In their brief return home they had managed to settle the children again and found friends who would lend them all the necessary goods until they returned from England. It was very sad to hear. Yet somehow Enoch and Phoebe managed to tell us with a smile on their faces.

It was, you will understand, rather embarrassing then to arrive at our home. We showed them their room with its comfy bed; the bathroom with its constant flow of hot and cold water; and the kitchen with all its pots, pans and electrical gadgets. Later, we rather sheepishly looked in our wardrobe at all our clothes. After they had settled themselves in their room they appeared downstairs. In her hands Phoebe held out a pot of groundnuts and some honey; 'For you, to say thank you for caring for us,' she said. The ground could have opened beneath me. Here were two people who had lost almost all of the very little that they possessed giving us a present. It remains one of the most generous acts we have ever experienced.

Over the years it is the poor of Uganda, Rwanda, Burundi and the south and east of London who have taught me most about generosity and not allowing money and possessions to dominate life. For money, and possessing more and more of this world's goods, brings many temptations. Indeed it was worry about these things which lay at the heart of Jesus' words that we considered in the last chapter. Now we focus specifically on the temptations that these things bring.

Happiness in possessing

One clear temptation of money is to think and believe that if only we had enough of it life would be happy and we would be content. Money certainly can, and does, bring some comfort into life. It enables us to enjoy a whole range of experiences that are not available to those who do not have it. Owning a home, international travel, theatre, dining out, having a PC in the home and owning an MP3 player are among the pleasures money can buy. But it certainly does not ultimately buy happiness. It is actually in talking with the really rich that this becomes clearest; those whom a friend described, when he was vicar of a very wealthy area in London, as 'the up and outs'. Money was no object for them. But their marriages were sometimes in a complete mess; some of their children were ruining their lives with addiction to heroin or cocaine; and their own mortality was beginning to hit them. 'I have everything I could ever want, yet my life is so empty,' one such person said.

Another way in which the temptation to believe that money brings happiness expresses itself is through the temptation of gambling. Playing the National Lottery; going for a big win on the horses; seeking a fortune through a spread bet or playing poker online are all expressions of hoping to win happiness. A wide range of activities in the stock market are simply a sophisticated form of gambling; particularly in areas like 'futures' markets. For many the weekly one or two pounds on the National Lottery or scratch cards or the occasional flutter at the bookies are largely harmless. The same, even more clearly, can be said of purchasing a few raffle tickets. However, for some gambling becomes a serious addiction. It causes major problems for the gambler and for their family as debts mount up. High-profile cases of massive gambling among sports stars, like those of the golfer John Daly and the footballer Wayne Rooney, are just the tip of the iceberg. Gambling is a major problem in our culture.

The temptation to believe that we can outwit the odds or find a quick solution through gambling is one that is very strong for some people. No one sets out to become a gambling addict; it starts for everyone in a small way but grows and develops until it becomes out of control. For those for whom it reaches such proportions, professional help and groups like Gamblers Anonymous are invaluable and essential. However, for most people the temptation of gambling is less strong but no less real. The straightforward resistance is to not indulge in any form of gambling at all. I have great sympathy with those who will not even buy a raffle ticket. Personally I have softened a little on this matter over the years; while not being a fan of raffles on odd occasions I will buy one. However, I remain firmly convinced that they have no place in church fundraising activities. Online gambling, through betting, poker games and the like, has developed dramatically in recent years. My simple advice is to avoid the temptation of becoming sucked into gambling this way by not becoming involved at all.

Involvement in the stock market raises a complexity of questions. Every one of us who has money in a bank and in a pension fund is an investor in the stock market. This is the way the financial systems work. There is here, I believe, a clear line to be drawn between investments and gambling. As all the adverts warn us in the small print, 'The value of investments can go down as well as up.' However, investment is done in good faith with a long-term view of benefiting both the company in which one invests and therefore oneself through a return on the investment. Hence wise, judicious investment seems to me to be justified. This historically is the basis on which the stock market has operated. However, there has been a growing trend towards a style of trading which is much more short term, and about making quick money at the expense of others. This turns the whole trading scene into a much greater gamble. It raises very serious questions about the ethics of such trading and leads to grave doubts about the appropriateness of these from a Christian angle. Too much trading of this sort seems to be at the expense of the poor and purely about financial gain for the few. Its focus is greed, not the good.

The temptation to believe that money can bring happiness is incredibly strong. It is strong because it contains within it some semblance of truth. Money does enable us to secure a more comfortable life. Money gives us the ability to have a good home in which to live; tasty, varied food to eat; and comfortable clothes to wear. It can buy us better education. It means that we can ensure better health of body and mind. It gives us the capacity to travel, to discover and to enjoy life. This is all true at a personal level. It is also true at the level of the community, society and nation. The wealthier a nation the greater capacity there is for all a nation's citizens to enjoy good housing, education and health. Yet money is not the source of true happiness. The temptation to believe that economic growth and development is all that is needed for a better world and the temptation to believe at a personal level that having more money will lead to greater happiness have both to be exposed for the lies that they really are.

Greed

Money tempts us into always wanting more. It pulls us into greed and covetousness (wanting for ourselves what belongs to someone else). This longing for more is not a purely personal one; it drives our culture and society. We have become completely wedded to a commitment to continual economic growth. We are driven not only by a desire to consume but also by a belief that consumption is the best way to live. 'I consume, therefore I am' appears to be the dominant philosophy of our day. Yet the evidence now all around us is shouting loudly that our consumption is keeping the majority of the world poor; further, our consumption is damaging the very planet on which we live, and cannot be sustained. In spite of the evidence it appears that we remain totally wedded to making and consuming more wealth. Contentment, once seen as a virtue, has become a dirty word.

This longing for more goods and desire for more money leads some to take for themselves through stealing. It leads to exploiting others in their earnings, and in trade systems so that some of us can have more at the expense of maintaining others in their poverty. Money, at least the love of it, tempts us into injustice and a decided lack of love for our neighbour, particularly the poor.

The love of money tempts us into jealousy of what others possess. Jealousy leads to the breakdown of relationships; even at extreme points to murder. What else is it other than greed and jealousy that leads to the organized armed robbery of millions of pounds from a bank? What other than greed and self-protection drives those who run the drugs trade, people-trafficking, organized prostitution and paedophilia around the globe? As the song from *Cabaret* goes, 'Money makes the world go round.' At least that is what money wants us to think, and how most of us live for much of the time.

Most of us can look on in judgement over those who engage in extreme crimes such as bank robbery and people-trafficking. This can lead us into thinking that we are innocent; we are okay. But the stark truth is that we are not okay. At all levels of life the temptations of money and possessions have an impact on us all.

I confess to having become increasingly angry with a line that, in parish life, I regularly heard from couples planning to marry. 'When will the wedding be?' I asked.

'Oh, not for at least two or three years,' came the cool reply. The couple were nearly always already living together, both were in work and they wanted to commit themselves to each other for the rest of their lives before God, his Church and their family and friends.

'Why so long a delay?' I innocently asked.

'Well, we can't afford the wedding yet,' came the regular reply, usually in a tone of 'Don't be so daft, mate, it's obvious, isn't it?'

The whole business has been completely turned on its head. Somewhere couples, following society's lead, think that a wedding must consist of a hugely expensive wedding dress, plus expensive bridesmaids' dresses; flowers galore; a photographer who will charge more than an arm and a leg, and often a video as well; two receptions (one for family and then an evening 'do' for all the friends) and then a hugely expensive honeymoon somewhere hot. Not to mention an expensive 'hen' and 'stag' night or weekend just before it all. All of this has to be in position it seems before the wedding can take place. Even though it means living together as man and wife for years before the celebration. I have pointed out on occasions that they could be married very simply just a few weeks later for not very much at all. Just occasionally (but very rarely) the point has been understood. Marriage is about the loving lifelong commitment of a woman and a man to each other within the life of the community; all the rest are mere trappings. Please do not misunderstand me. Celebrating marriage is great. Gathering the family and friends together to share in the ceremony and joy of it all are important. But, somehow, we have turned the wedding celebration into some kind of idol and forgotten the heart of what the marriage ceremony and covenant are all about.

Then the desire for more money, to provide an ever larger home and more and more goods within it, drives both partners to work harder and harder at their jobs. They work so hard that time to be with one another can be squeezed out, and the relationship is not nurtured. This failure to nurture the relationship can easily lead into affairs, disillusionment and the break-up of the relationship.

But many marriages do last. A child comes along. Thankfully we are beginning to see some return of recognition that parental care is crucial in the earliest days, months and years of life. There is greater encouragement for both parents to take time out from work to care as mother and as father. But couples are putting off having children, 'Until we are a little more financially secure', or 'Just while I develop my career'. Couples are also more frequently deciding to have only one or at most two children, 'Because we can't afford more'. Those who decide to limit their family size because of the world population have more sympathy from me but to do so for economic reasons seems to me to turn the child more into an economic commodity. Or at least it shows a conviction that possessing things and having certain experiences that cost money is what makes for a full and happy childhood.

For far too many people the marriage relationship, becoming and being parents, and the whole experience of childhood is being dictated by convictions about money and possessions rather than by loving relationships. Acting responsibly and thoughtfully in relationships is vital. Considering the proper care and nurture of children is essential. This must include some thought about money. But when money and economics take over from love, care, kindness, time and patience then something has gone very wrong with our priorities and understanding about relationships and parenthood. We have succumbed to money's tempting lie that it is the one we should serve.

Self-sufficiency

The heart of money's power of temptation is that it pulls us away from the living God. It leads us down the road into greed, jealousy, injustice, exploitation, theft and even the destruction of life. Above all else, wealth and success tempt us into a conviction that we are, and can be, self-sufficient. They lead us into individualism and a personal private world in which we think that we do not need others; or that others are there for our benefit. We lose the idea of community and the common good. Love of money leads us into a conviction that we do not need God. This is no new temptation; it was the stern warning given to the Israelites about life in the Promised Land (Deuteronomy 8); it was the observation of the Psalmist (Psalm 73) and the warning of the prophets (see Isaiah's warning to Babylon, Isaiah 47). Little wonder then that Jesus, who saw his ministry as fulfilling the Law and the Prophets, said, 'You cannot serve God and Wealth' (Matthew 6.24).

Jesus and money

Sometimes the Church is accused of being obsessed with money. On occasions this accusation has validity. However, the same accusation could be made at Jesus. He very regularly talked about money and wealth. He was deeply conscious of the many temptations which come with wealth. If we look at Luke's Gospel we can note initially part of Mary's Song (known by many as the Magnificat) in which she says of God, 'He has filled the hungry with good things, and sent the rich away empty' (Luke 1.53); the way Jesus is tempted in the wilderness with food, wealth and power (Luke 4.1–13), and Jesus' use of Isaiah to be the manifesto for his ministry including 'good news to the poor' (Luke 4.18 quoting Isaiah

61.1–2). There then comes the call of Levi the tax collector (Luke 5.27–32). The first piece of specific teaching on money quoted by Luke comes in the 'Sermon on the Plain', 'Blessed are you who are poor . . . But woe to you who are rich, for you have received your consolation' (Luke 6.20–26). Further challenges follow on the cost of being a disciple of Jesus in relation to status and security. Then we arrive at the parable of the rich fool in Luke 12.13f. followed by teaching about food, clothing and anxiety. There is the parable of the shrewd manager in Luke 16.1f.; the story of the rich man and Lazarus in 16.19f.; then the story of the rich young ruler in 18.22–25; Zacchaeus in 19.1–10 and the widow and her offering in 21.1–4. Jesus is very clear indeed through all of these that there is a real temptation to build up wealth for ourselves. He is clear that greed is a serious issue. He is also clear that there is a temptation to build our security in money and property rather than in God and his kingdom. Jesus warns us sternly, and demonstrates through his life that the Father does supply all needs. Jesus shows us a way of dependence and faith.

Now all of this teaching certainly indicates Jesus' own awareness of the reality of the temptations which come with money and wealth. I am sure that we can safely assume that before he ever entered his public ministry he experienced these temptations for himself in his world of work as a carpenter. He surely wrestled with the temptation not to leave home at all, but to stay and provide for the family and live a straightforward life in Nazareth. Yet he knew that the Father's kingdom and justice had to take priority. Even though this meant leaving for a life of simplicity; a life in which he had nowhere to lay his head; a life when sometimes it was uncertain where the next meal would come from; a life dependent on God rather than money. When Jesus taught his disciples to pray, 'Give us each day our daily bread' (Luke 11.3) he was sharing with them his own prayer based on his own experience of his Father. Jesus, it appears, did not pray for long-term monetary provision or great storehouses of wealth. He simply prayed for the needs of each day as it came.

I often ponder what Jesus would say to us about our obsession with pension policies and plans; insurance policies for everything and our savings accounts (for a rainy day). I do not conclude that he would tell us to drop and abandon them all but he would surely challenge our dependence on them and our obsession with trying to make ourselves as secure as possible against every last eventuality. He would challenge us to rely on God, trust him, and seek his kingdom and justice first; all else must come under that governance. I write 'what would he say' but in the words and stories from the Gospels he does speak to us now. We do not have to imagine what he would say if he were here. He is present and speaking through his living word.

We all need to heed Jesus' warning and learn to live light to our possessions knowing that they are all temporary. We need to learn a spirit of generosity which will allow us to let go, and give away rather than grasp and hoard. We need to recover an attitude of dependence on the Father. Careful, thoughtful planning for the future, especially providing for our families, seems entirely godly; so pension provision for what we need and life insurance policies make sense. But do we really need pensions for our wants? Is it really necessary to insure everything against every eventuality? Surely the needs of the poor come before a host of appliance insurance policies.

We need to learn repentance for our false worship of money; for our greed and covetousness; for our faith in it to give us security. This repentance must show itself in changed lifestyles; ones in which we live more simply, more contentedly and marked by generosity. Lives in which we truly recognize that our lives now and for eternity are in God's hands, not our own. Lives in which we serve God rather than money.

Ideas for reflection

1 How do the temptations of money show themselves in your life?
2 Are there actions you could take to loosen money's hold over you?

3 What might contented living look like in our postmodern
  society?

Pictures

Jesus Mafa: *Rich Fool*; *Widow's Mite*; *Zacchaeus*
Sidney Spencer: *Consider the Lilies* or *The Foxes have Holes*

Prayer

Lord God, owner of all things,
two things I ask of you;
do not deny them to me before I die:
Remove far from me falsehood and lying;
give me neither poverty nor riches;
feed me with the food that I need,
or I shall be full and deny you,
and say, 'Who is the LORD?'
or I shall be poor, and steal,
and profane the name of my God.

(All but the first line from the Prayer of Agur
Proverbs 30.7–9)

7

Pride and humility

It was my final night leading the camp at Longbarn Meadow, near Tonbridge, Kent. I was feeling very emotional. After 30 years of involvement I now had to step down. My dear friends Geoff and Sarah, with whom I had worked on the camp for 11 years, put together a wonderful farewell and thanks. Tears flowed as we planted 'TP' (my camp nickname) and Rosemary's oak by the stream.

It had all begun for me in the mid-1970s as an 18-year-old. A holiday club in Borstal, Kent, was my first working experience with Scripture Union evangelist Dai Lewis. Joining him at the new camps he was holding in a field with no facilities at Carroty Wood just seemed to be a natural development. At the end of my first summer Dai asked me if I would return the following year in a more clearly 'leading' role. I readily agreed. He and Maureen were wonderful to work with; the camps were huge fun and I enjoyed working with the age group (8 to 11). Neither he, nor I, imagined that the association would be as long as it has proved to be. John Horne, the owner of Carroty Woods, began to see the huge possibilities of the site and through the Barnabas Trust began to develop the area until today Carroty Woods is one of the best camping centres for children and young people in the south-east of England. The development, however, did not quite fit with the ethos that Dai and Maureen had sought to create. John Horne recognized this and offered the Lewises a piece of woodland and field just a mile up the road. With enormous vision, and a huge amount of hard work, this site developed into Longbarn Meadow, where since 1981 Longbarn camps have been based. The memories of the excitement of those years of development still bring a tingle down my spine.

In 1987, encouraged by Cathie Smith and Janet Morgan, Rosemary and I began a specific camp for children from Tower Hamlets. We worked in close partnership with a small number of local churches. In 1987 just 17 children came; it was the hardest camp of our lives! It was this camp to which I had to say farewell on moving to the Diocese of Winchester. I hope that someday someone will manage to write a brief history of Longbarn for it has been a remarkable ministry. The Lewis family still run four weeks of camps every summer. The East End week continues. These camps have shaped and changed many lives – those of children and of leaders. They have helped children discover more about themselves, about nature, about relationships with peers and adults, about living in community and about God in Jesus Christ. I am proud of having been a part of it; and for such a long period of time. Longbarn camps have been an immense achievement. They have been one of the most significant parts of my life.

Now there's the rub in the story: I am proud of the achievement. Actually there are many things of which I am proud. I am proud of my four children; they are wonderful people. I am proud of Rosemary; she is an amazing wife, mother, children's worker, craft-worker and Christian. I am proud of how people with whom I have been engaged in ministry in a variety of churches have come to faith, grown in discipleship and developed in Christian ministry. But isn't pride a sin? Should I feel and think this way about such matters in my life? There is plenty for which I feel ashamed. I have a vast catalogue of failures but of the achievements I do have some real sense of pride – should I do so? And if there is any right sense of pride, what moves that into being wrong and harmful?

Correct assessment

The problem may lie in our use of the words 'pride' and 'proud'. The most famous falsely humble person in English literature is Charles Dickens' loathsome character Uriah Heep, the servant who is always 'ever so 'umble'. In reality he was exactly the opposite: full of himself, not really respecting others and continually scheming to put, or bring, others down and raise himself up. The 'pride' which is sin is haughtiness, self-exaltation and arrogance. Adam and Eve's pride in the Genesis story is their thinking that they knew better than God, which leads them into disobedience.

However, when we talk about being 'proud' of our children, or even of some of our life's achievements we can be talking about a right and proper assessment of their and our gifts. We are one of those families who produce a 'round robin' Christmas letter. It is, for us, a good way of keeping in touch with our friends and relatives across the country and the globe. We appreciate receiving them from others because we like to hear news and have a sense of staying in touch, even if the demands of life make it difficult to actually meet up very often. However, there is a clear danger with these letters of creating a competitive spirit, of seeing who can outdo each other for the children's exam results or the places we have visited through the year. We are very grateful for the letters we receive which are self-deprecating and humorous about family failures. These letters, which some hate, demonstrate something of the fine line between making a fair, honest and genuine assessment of achievements or becoming arrogant and self-promoting. It would be false to pretend, for example, that my children achieved worse grades than they actually did in their exams. But it might well be that the 'C' grade was the greatest achievement because of all that had gone into it; in a world obsessed with academic league tables this might be hard to convey.

The temptation of pride then is to make of ourselves more than we should. It can express itself in both arrogance and false humility, pretending that we are less than we actually are. The godly art is to learn to think of ourselves neither more highly than we ought, nor less than we ought. As St Paul put it, 'For by the grace given to me I say to everyone among you not to think of yourself more highly than you ought to think, but to think with sober judgement, each according to the measure of faith that God has assigned' (Romans 12.3).

In these verses Paul immediately goes on to talk about the gifts God has given each of us within the body of Christ. It is right to accept, recognize and use the gifts that God has given us. To accept that we have a gift of hospitality, or of leading, or of teaching is not to be proud but to simply recognize God's grace at work within us. Pride comes in when we start regarding 'our' gift as being more important or significant than those of others. Pride comes in when we start regarding ourselves as being more 'spiritual' or 'blessed' because we have a particular gift and others do not have it.

It is false humility to deny a gift that we have been given, or to try and pretend that we are not gifted by God in a particular way. God gives us different gifts to use for the good of all; when we try and pretend that we are less than we are, we are as guilty of false humility as the person who overblows their own trumpet is of pride. We are in this together and must help each other make a correct assessment of our gifts and calling under God. We have to honour one another above ourselves. It is essential that we recognize, honour and encourage the use of gifts in, and by, each other. We really do need to admit to one another within the body of Christ that everyone matters and that we are mutually interdependent. The same applies within society and humanity as a whole. Pride leads us into independence, disagreements, arguments and conflicts.

Jesus, the humble servant

Jesus was at dinner with a leading Pharisee and many guests. Jesus, ever watchful of people's behaviour, noticed how as the guests arrived for the meal they chose the seats of honour. They wished to be close to the action; they wanted to be seen to be important. So he told a parable about a wedding feast and the huge embarrassment of the man who sat in a seat of honour only to be publicly humiliated by being moved elsewhere when a more important guest arrived. Jesus closes the parable with the words, 'For all who exalt themselves will be humbled, and those who humble themselves will be exalted' (Luke 14.11). This would appear to be a phrase that was something of a refrain in Jesus' teaching (Matthew 23.12). Arguments about greatness, status and privilege arose among the disciples on several occasions throughout the three years that they travelled with Jesus. Jesus' response time and again was to point them towards humility and service. On one occasion James and John, along with their mother, request the best seats of authority in heaven. This causes uproar among their colleagues. Jesus speaks to them not of power over others but of service, humility and suffering (Mark 10.35–45). Even during the last supper an argument about greatness arises; Jesus adopts the role of the servant and washes the disciples' feet to show them that true greatness lies in service (Luke 22.24–27; John 13).

Jesus was tempted to self-exaltation and pride. In the wilderness Satan urges him to display his power before the people; during his ministry his unbelieving brothers encourage him to a public display of power (John 7.1–5) and right at the end he is urged to display his power by climbing down from the cross and proving his power to all (Mark 15.31–32). How often, I wonder, in the quiet of an evening, the throng of the crowd, or facing the taunts of the Pharisees, did Jesus find himself thinking, 'I'll show them. They want to see power. I'll give them some they will never forget.' Yet not once did he succumb to the temptation to put himself above the Father's will. At every step of the way he chose humility, service and a proper self-assessment of who he was and to what he was called.

If ever a man had things of which he could boast and be proud it was Jesus; all those healings and miracles; all those changed lives. But in him there is found no arrogance.

How did he do this? He was clear that he did nothing alone; he relied on his Father's power and wisdom: 'Very truly, I tell you, the Son can do nothing on his own, but only what he sees the Father doing' (John 5.19). He lived in dependence on the Holy Spirit. His focus was always the Father's will and glory: 'My food is to do the will of him who sent me and to complete his work' (John 4.34).

Jesus knew exactly who he was, what the Father had called him to do and the power with which he would achieve it. Each step of the way he had to discern the right thing to do so that he would fulfil the Father's total will. There is no arrogance because he is doing what he is called to do, no more and no less. There is no false humility because he knows his identity and his destiny so he can rest secure in both.

Our constant wrestling

Pride, it appears, comes into our lives because of our desire to assert ourselves among, and indeed over and above others. Our failure to be fully secure in our identity leads us to either overestimate our worth and achievements, or to underestimate them. Overestimation leads to arrogance. Underestimation leads to a wrong humility because it undervalues who we are as a person made in God's likeness, loved deeply by him, and accepted as his child.

My own experience is that I wrestle continually with both temptations. On the one hand I am tempted to be arrogant and think of myself more highly than I should; to try and make myself out to be better than others, better than I really am. It is so tempting to think that my gifts and my ministry are more valuable or important than those of others; I am even encouraged, on occasions, to think that way by others within the Church. Yet a right assessment is that my gifts are no more important than those of others and my calling is no more vital than that of any other within the body of Christ. I am called to be faithful with the gifts and responsibilities I have been given in exactly the same way as every other follower of Jesus. In the parable of the talents Jesus makes it quite clear that it is faithfulness in service which counts, not the quantity of achievement (Matthew 25.14–30).

On the other hand I am tempted, at times, to see myself as worthless, valueless and useless. Indeed such thoughts regularly assail me. Yet the truth is that God has made me in his image; he loves me, and the world, so much that he gave his one and only Son for us; he has, in Jesus Christ, rescued and redeemed me and adopted me as his child. He has poured out his Holy Spirit upon me and given me gifts. If God thinks this highly of each of us, how dare we undervalue ourselves and one another?

The answer to both pride and false humility then is to be like Jesus himself; to rest secure in who God has made me to be and to seek to do only that for which he has gifted, equipped and empowered me. The journey to that place of complete security, and therefore an end to pride, and a proper humility, will go on until the day of my death; but it is a journey worth taking.

Ideas for reflection

1 Trying to be honest with yourself, do you tend towards arrogance or false humility?
2 Of what can you be rightly 'proud'?
3 Talk with others about a right assessment of your own abilities.

Pictures

Jesus Mafa: *Pharisee and Publican* and *Washing Feet*
Dinah Roe Kendall: *Jesus Washing the Disciples' Feet*
Sidney Spencer: *Rising from Sleep in the Morning*

Prayer

Lord, I can be so proud and stubborn. Teach me true humility that I might truly know whose I am and whom I serve. I pray in the name of the one who humbled himself even to death on the cross, Jesus Christ my Lord. Amen.

8

Power and service

————◆◆————

It was obvious what was going on. There in the midst of a church council meeting two strong-willed characters with determined opinions about styles of how the church's ministry of healing should be conducted were seeking to manoeuvre people into supporting their own view. I sat back to watch. It was fascinating and intriguing to observe the changing physical postures of the two protagonists. The use of words and, more importantly, the use of tone and inflection in the voice were dynamic. All around the room it was possible to observe others shifting their support one way and then the other. While many chipped into the discussion it was clear that the focus lay on the two main players. I let the discussion run; I encouraged it; I watched it. Then suddenly it hit me. There was a third powerful player engaged in this discussion; I was no neutral observer, as I kept suggesting to myself; I was actually the one holding the reins of power. I was after all 'in the chair'. I was the one allowing, even encouraging, the debate to run as it was doing. It was clear that all were looking to me to keep hold of the reins so that everyone was heard fairly, had a chance to speak and to listen. I was no neutral observer but one of the power players. The sudden realization reminded me that I had to fulfil my role carefully and thoughtfully and that I had better stop the self-indulgent enjoyment of watching and analysing the debate taking place before me, instructive and entertaining though it was.

Power is being exercised all the time, in all of life's settings. Walk into a classroom and observe the power of the teacher being exercised in relation to the children of the class. Watch also the power games played by the pupils in relation to the teacher and to one another. Go then into the playground and watch the power relationships at work between children, and groups of children. Join the staff at their after-school meeting and observe the power plays that take place between the various staff members present. It is not always the most vocal or forceful, or even those whose title suggests power, that actually exercise their power most successfully. Switch to an office setting and observe; very quickly you will see how the power is being exercised by 'bosses' over their staff, by peers over each other, and sometimes by the staff over their boss. Ricky Gervais' classic comedy series, *The Office*, demonstrates this again and again both very humorously and also very insightfully.

When we talk of 'power' we can very quickly leap into thinking about those whom we deem powerful in our world; the Presidents of the USA and China; the Prime Minister and members of the Government; the leaders of 'big corporate business'; media magnates; and perhaps the forces of law and order. Certainly in reflecting on the temptations of power we must consider these. However, it is how we exercise power where we are, with the people with whom we deal most of the time that I want to focus on primarily. How we exercise power in our workplaces, our homes, our local church and our community groups is where, for most of us, most of the time, the real temptations and tests will arise.

Power looks very attractive most of the time.

Parents have a great deal of power over their children. They can use this power lovingly to care for the children, and seek the best for them. But there are times when all parents are tempted to misuse the power they have over their child(ren). So the temptation, on occasions, will be to use the power of the louder voice to shout a child down; or the power of having a greater vocabulary to twist and turn an argument with a child. The power of the parent's physical presence, let alone the temptation to use physical force to get a child to comply, is one which the parent, or carer, knows only too well. They must always be aware of such power and of the temptation to misuse it.

I am nearly six foot three inches tall. I will never forget the time that I was standing at the front of a primary-school assembly with the reception children sitting cross-legged at my feet; all was quiet as I began. I asked a question and one brave reception child in front of me raised her arm; I bent down to ask for her answer. 'Are you a giant?' she said.

The school laughed; I smiled. It was not what I had been expecting but it told me a great deal about what was going on in that child's mind. I stayed crouched down and said, 'No, I'm not a giant but I guess that sitting where you are and looking up at me I might look like one.'

'Yes,' came the confident reply; but rather gratifyingly it was followed by, 'but I think you're a nice giant.'

I cannot remember what the assembly was about but I remember the conversation because it taught me a great deal about how young children see me, and how to be very aware of my physical 'power' in such a setting.

Parental and adult power is but one example; we have already noted the power that bosses can wield over their staff rather than serving them for the best for the firm and the staff.

Professionals such as doctors, social workers, counsellors and the police all possess significant power over others within their professional settings. Great care must always be exercised by such professionals because there will always be points at which the temptation to misuse or abuse power over a patient or client will be very strong.

Christian ministers and pastors can wield power over their congregations rather than serving them. The pulpit can be misused and abused as a tool of power by the preacher. Strong worship leaders, using the emotional power of music, their position and the power of visual images, can misuse the power placed in their hands. Elders, deacons and churchwardens can all be guilty of misusing their position and power. So can bishops.

Politicians at all levels have power but those in the highest offices have a great deal of power. So do the leaders of major industries.

Power is seductive. The temptation of power is to use it for one's own ends. The test with power is how to use it for the glory of God and the good of others. The question that we always have to ask is, 'How can I use the power that I have to serve rather than be served?'

Jesus and power – the wilderness temptations

All three of Jesus' temptations in the wilderness relate in one way or another to the use and abuse of power. If we take the order in Matthew's Gospel, the first temptation relates to using his power to satisfy his own bodily needs and wants; the second is a temptation to make a display of power to win people over by dazzling them with a dramatic leap from the top of the Temple; the third wilderness temptation is to grasp political power and splendour by bowing down to the devil (Matthew 4.2–10). There is no disagreement by Jesus with the devil's suggestion that he does have the authority and power to do all three things. Neither does Jesus disagree with the devil that he has power in the earth and its nations; a truth that we would do well not to forget.

In response to all three 'power' temptations, Jesus does not enter into a theological debate with the devil about food, the power of angels nor even about the earth and everything in it belonging to the Lord. He could have done this. Instead in all three instances he goes to the heart of the matter. Who do I worship and obey? Power is to be exercised in response to this question. How we use whatever power we have reveals how we are answering this question for ourselves.

The devil invites Jesus to worship him. Jesus responds each time with a Scripture quotation (all from Deuteronomy: 8.3; 6.6, 13). Worship and obedience, Jesus is making clear, belong truly only to the Lord God. Power is to be used only in ways which express worship and obedience to God. Power is not to be used merely for personal fulfilment, gratification or aggrandizement.

The Israelites in the wilderness had given in to the temptation to worship false gods. They had made the image of the golden calf and abandoned the Lord. The words Jesus quotes from Deuteronomy are words relating to their life in the wilderness and their future in the Promised Land. Moses' words are to say that as God's people they must depend on God and worship and serve him only. Jesus knew their history; he knew that they had failed to do so and had fallen into worshipping all kinds of false gods. But he now chooses the way of the Lord and will not bow the knee to anyone or anything other than the Lord himself. He refuses the way of misusing his power or seeking overt political power. He chooses the way of humility in worship and service.

We will never face the choice of ruling the whole world. But in our own ways we will face the temptations of power. We will face the temptations to worship others, or other things, rather than God himself.

Just as the children of Israel fell prey to false worship so can we. We worship the gods of Money, Security, Family, Success and Fame. We show our worship by serving them; using our energies, time and money towards them rather than towards the living God. Our idols are often far more subtle than the idols of ancient Canaan but they are just as real. Beware the temptation to think that we don't have idols today.

The contrast between the devil and Jesus in the third temptation is simple and clear. The devil sought to be served. The Son of God sought to be the Servant. The devil craved to be worshipped. The Son wanted to be a Worshipper. Christians are called to be like Jesus. We are called to worship and serve the one true God.

The power of popularity

We know that Jesus became extremely, though not universally, popular. Crowds flocked to see him, and to follow him around. This popularity meant Jesus was also growing in the possibility of people power. He could influence and lead them. John's account

of the feeding of the 5,000 gives us an insight into the possibilities that were arising (John 6.1–15). The people want to make Jesus
King, by force. Jesus sees this and refuses to go this way. He recognizes the same temptation that had confronted him in the wilderness. The way of popularity and power was not the way to do the
Father's will and bring in the kingdom. God's kingdom is of a very
different order.

We see this temptation again several times over in the
Pharisees' requests for Jesus to 'give them a sign' (Luke 11.16, 29;
Matthew 12.38; 16.1; Mark 8.11). They want a big demonstration
of divine power. But Jesus refuses to go this route. It must have
been tempting to prove them wrong. But Jesus knew that the Father's
way was the way of undergoing God's judgement on human
rebellion through his death and burial.

Most people will never face the potential for such huge popularity and the consequent people power that confronted Jesus
(though it is a temptation that does come the way of some politicians and media stars). Nevertheless, the temptation to use what
power we have to please others and to gain popularity within our
own circles of influence will be real for all of us. The natural-born
comic can use wit and humour to win friends and become the
centre of attention. Gifted organizers can skilfully manoeuvre a group
of people into agreeing with their way of doing things. There is
nothing wrong with popularity per se. Some people, by their very
nature, will prove to be popular. However, if we simply court popularity for its own sake, or to make us feel better about ourselves
then we are giving in to the temptation to place ourselves at the
centre of things rather than God. Popularity always needs to be
placed under the spotlight of God's glory. If the popularity arises
through fulfilling God's purposes then we can and should accept
it. However, it must always be offered back to God for his glory.
For Jesus there was the need never to allow his popularity to divert
him from his call.

This is clearly seen in another incident in the Gospels, found
in Luke 4.42f. and Mark 1.35f. These are the early days of Jesus'

public ministry and he is proving to be very popular and successful. In this situation the temptation was to stay put; to enjoy the success and perhaps settle for the comfort and ease of it. But Jesus refuses to stay, settle down or live with the success. He knows that the Father has a wider role and ministry for him. He knows that he has a responsibility to proclaim the good news to other communities as well. So he resists the temptation to stay, and moves on.

Popularity will always hold the temptation of becoming comfortable, and of overestimating ourselves. It will always contain within it the temptation to misuse the power over others that it brings. Our resistance lies in our decision not to be led or driven by popularity, but rather by doing the will of God, which can lead us into some very unpopular places.

Power for good

Power, then, is something every one of us possesses in some situations. Our first task might be to actually recognize the power that we have; in our homes, our workplaces and our churches. This power comes from our positions, our personalities and our responsibilities. There is absolutely nothing wrong with having power; it is God-given. But the temptations to misuse and abuse power are enormous. We can use power to put ourselves at the centre and to gain personal advantage. This is a strong and seductive temptation that never leaves us. Yet the calling of the most powerful man who ever lived is to lay down power in the service of others; to use whatever power we have for the glory of God through seeking the good of others, especially our 'enemies'. The best way to use power is to surrender it to God.

Ideas for reflection

1 In what situations do you hold some power? What temptations to misuse it come your way?
2 Can you think of examples of people using their power well?
3 How might you use your power more like Christ?

Pictures

Jesus Mafa: *Stilling the Storm* or *Feeding of 5,000* and *Washing Feet*
Dinah Roe Kendall: *Washing Feet*
Sidney Spencer: *The Scorpion*

Prayer

God, we call you Almighty, all-powerful. You use your power to
create, to uphold, to serve. Help me to recognize the power you
have given me. Give me the wisdom I need to use that power
to serve you by serving others. Amen.

9

Violence and peace

———◆◆———

Ever since Mark Adams nearly knocked me out in a boxing contest at Scout Cubs when we were 10 years old I have not really liked violence. At least I do not like the thought of being personally involved with it, either by being on the receiving end or administering it. However, I do sometimes watch it. I watch it on the news, in sport (officially in boxing and unofficially in a punch-up on the rugby field) and in TV programmes and films. Personally very violent acts sicken me. Yet I am fascinated by TV and films that involve solving murders that are often horrific (take *Messiah* and *Waking the Dead* as two examples). Then there was a moment of intense personal disgust when I realized that I was actually enjoying watching the news footage of bombs falling on Iraq. How could I be 'enjoying' the destruction, violence and death that this entailed? Ever since I have tried to consciously remind myself of the reality on the ground of what war means for the victims, however, much I can marvel at the technical 'brilliance' of modern weaponry, the skill of pilots, the discipline of soldiers and the tactical skills of military commanders.

Yet 'soft', 'placid' and 'docile' as I am by character there can be times when an inner rage erupts which wants to let itself out in some violent way. Very often my way of expressing this is through words. I can honestly say that I have never physically assaulted anyone (I don't think I landed one successful punch on Mark Adams in my one and only boxing bout!). But I have certainly been guilty of verbal assaults, sadly sometimes on those nearest and dearest to me. I am quite good with words and arguments and in some settings I know that I have the capacity to embarrass someone else by making them look stupid or small. It is a temptation that has to be resisted.

My ministry has meant that I have met many who have been the victims of violence; child abuse, domestic violence, rape, mugging, physical assault, suicide, war and murder all included. This involves people in the UK, USA, Peru, Uganda, Rwanda, Sudan, Ivory Coast, South Africa, Zimbabwe, Russia, Iran, Pakistan, Burma/Myanmar, and Australia. As a family we have experienced a family member being mugged, threats of physical attack, violent verbal assault, and the violence of having a home ransacked through burglary. We have lost a good friend through murder.

My ministry has also meant involvement with a wide range of professionals and volunteers who work with both the victims and perpetrators of violence; these include doctors, nurses, social workers, community and youth workers, police, undertakers and counsellors. One Sunday evening after the church service ended a young man joined us as we drank coffee. He was clearly uneasy and disturbed. He asked if he could talk with me. As we sat quietly in the side aisle of the church (with a churchwarden judiciously finding lots of tidying up to do elsewhere in the building but always in sight) John (not his real name) poured out his tale of violence. He had physically assaulted his girlfriend. Could he be forgiven? Over the following months we met several times and the tales of violence came out. He had committed most violent crimes you could imagine, except murder. He had served some time inside for grievous bodily harm. But now he wanted to change, yet the violent urges still came, the red mist still descended. As is usually the case he was himself a victim of violence. Both parents had abused him as a child, physically, sexually, verbally and emotionally. The only language he had learned to express anger or even disagreement was violence. I wept for him, and with him. We prayed together. He started reading the Bible and discovered a world of violent people whom God had not abandoned but loved, forgave and used. He went for professional counselling and became deeply engaged in community activity. He even managed to talk with his parents about the past; though they did not want to listen or acknowledge the truth. He was making immense progress in understanding that God's love does forgive violence of all kinds. Formal church activity was difficult for him but Jesus Christ was real in his life. Then he suddenly disappeared. I have no idea where John is today but I often pray for him. John's experience, and perpetration, of violence is at one extreme end but the reality is that all of us experience violence in some way or another, and all of us are tempted to commit some kind of violence.

Rosemary and I say that we could never understand why anyone would hurt a child until we had one who would not sleep at night. As we became more and more tired and the weeks went on we scared ourselves with the realization that there were moments when the temptation to do something violent for a few moments' peace was very strong. We both understand how easy it is for someone to suddenly 'snap' and hit a child harder than intended, causing them serious damage. For some, once that line has been crossed it seems to be easier to cross it again and again.

'Jane' suffered a great deal as a child. She was physically and sexually abused by her father. Through years of prayer, counselling and therapy she has developed into a well-matured adult. Yet the 'worst' violence she has sometimes suggested was that done by her primary school teacher. With her self-worth already diminished by her father's behaviour, school was the one place where she hoped to be accepted and valued. Instead she found herself being called 'not very clever, and stupid'. She can remember a teacher saying, 'Well, you'll never be very clever so don't worry about trying too hard.' She remembers the words because they stung her into fulfilling them. She developed a reputation for laziness, poor behaviour and 'being stupid'. Somewhere inside her she knew this was not true. In adulthood she increasingly realized that she was cleverer than she had been told. She began studying and now holds a master's degree. She gives her life to helping victims of abuse. Hers is not an isolated story; another friend with a not dissimilar background now holds a doctorate. It was the combination of violence which restricted and stultified the development and growth of these two women but both, intriguingly, point to the verbal violence by parent and teacher that caused the most damage and took the most time from which to recover.

Their story is at an extreme end but it makes the point clear; verbal violence is damaging. We are all tempted to engage in this in a whole variety of ways; name-calling, spiteful words, character assassination, giving false hope, flattery and a host of other techniques flow from our mouths to assault, hurt and damage another. 'Sticks and stones may break my bones but words will never hurt me' has to be one of the most incorrect proverbial statements ever uttered.

Jesus and violence

James and John, whose nickname was 'sons of thunder', thought that violence would be a good way of dealing with the Samaritan village that refused to offer hospitality to Jesus and his friends (Luke 9.51–55). They might well have thought that they had good precedent in Elijah the prophet's actions (2 Kings 1.9–15). But Jesus rebuked them firmly for making such a violent suggestion. The temptation was put in his way and he refused it.

When Jesus was arrested in the Garden of Gethsemane, Peter drew a sword and cut off Malchus' ear. It was an understandable reaction. Peter wants to defend his Master. He also wants to prove Jesus wrong in his prediction that Peter would deny Jesus. But Jesus knew that this was not the way to fulfil his Father's will. Jesus made it clear that there was an option for him to choose to use overwhelming force; he could have called on legions of angels to protect him and fight for him (Matthew 26.53). But this was not the way the Father had called him to go. So he resisted the temptation to take the way of violence.

This reflected his teaching that it is the peacemakers who are blessed (Matthew 5.9) and that murder begins with anger in the heart (Matthew 5.21–22; Mark 7.21).

Jesus also knew the temptation of verbal violence. He talked of malice coming from within the heart (Mark 7.22, NIV). He also deliberately chose not to indulge in verbal attack or retaliation with Judas, his betrayer, or his accusers. How tempting it must have been for Jesus to get his own back; one retaliatory word whispered in response. One small spit back. One harsh word shouted at a tormentor. He is provoked and goaded again and again – by the Sanhedrin first, then by the soldiers and then by all the mockers around the cross. But not one word of retaliation comes. As Peter wrote, recalling the words of Isaiah 53,

> 'He committed no sin, and no deceit was found in his mouth.' When he was abused, he did not return abuse; when he suffered he did not threaten; but he entrusted himself to the one who judges justly.
>
> (1 Peter 2.22–23)

I just do not know how he did it. I cannot get my head around how he was able to withstand such temptation. But he did.

The temptation to retaliate – particularly with words – can be very, very strong. We have to learn to resist it. We need to learn to bite our tongues rather than retaliate.

The way of violence at times is a temptation for the follower of Jesus:

- The parent so distraught with their child, and perhaps so weary, that the quickest solution seems to be a sharp slap. Violence takes the place of love.
- The anger that builds up inside with someone for their unreasonable behaviour which we think we can sort 'with a good thumping'.

Then there are the Christians who are so upset by the scandal of the ease of abortions that they resort to violence against abortion clinics and their staff in the USA. Or those who feel so deeply that some shows are blasphemous (e.g. *Jerry Springer The Opera* and *Romans in Britain*) that they seek to physically stop people entering the shows. Or those who are so concerned with the power of big business and the forces of globalization that they believe they must demonstrate to the G8 Leaders or gatherings of the World Trade Organization and, while doing so, attack the police and destroy property. The concern for justice for the unborn is right and proper; the sentiments about particular plays may have validity; and the passion for trade justice is certainly correct – but there can be no justification for resorting to violence as a means of protest. Violence will always be counterproductive. Jesus chose the way of non-violence. He calls his followers to do the same.

When the temptation to resort to violence comes we may need to find a displacement activity to let off steam. Hitting a cushion or a wall is certainly better than hitting a child. Going and smashing a squash ball all around a court has to be preferable to 'taking it out' on a fellow human being. Going for a run, or a long walk, allowing the energy to be used elsewhere can help. So too can simply finding space and stillness. Prayer, even shouting at God and venting our anger on him is okay – after all, the Psalms are filled with such words. I have often preached and talked about Jesus taking time alone with his Father in prayer to listen to the Father's will and discern the way ahead. Might it also be that this is where Jesus took his frustrations and temptations to respond angrily or maliciously towards his slow-to-learn disciples and vicious detractors? He knew the Psalms well enough to quote Psalm 22 as he hung upon the cross. Might he not have used some of the Psalms of anger and doubt to express his feelings when alone with his Father? I think it highly likely.

There was, notably, one occasion when Jesus did seem to use violence. (Or possibly two if John 2.13–17 refers to an incident near the outset of his ministry.) This was when he entered the Temple in Jerusalem and overthrew the money changers' tables and drove out the sheep and the goats (Matthew 21.12–13; Mark

11.15–18; Luke 19.45–46). We need to understand the context. This incident took place in the Court of the Gentiles. Jewish worshippers coming to offer sacrifices at the Temple were forced to change their money into 'temple money' in order to purchase the sheep, goats and birds on sale here. The whole thing had become a religious scam. Ordinary people it seems were being ripped off through the money-changing scheme and then forced into buying the animals from here rather than bringing their own. So worship and prayer had been turned into a profit-making deal. What made it even worse was that by conducting all of this in the one area of the Temple open to all peoples from any nation and of whatever faith these very 'people of the nations' were effectively being excluded. So Jesus' fury (we cannot call it anything less) was at the degrading of prayer and worship which was taking place. He wanted to remove all of this activity so that the Temple could be used as it was meant to be, 'a house of prayer for all nations'. Jesus' act is a prophetic statement. It does involve some action which appears violent – making a whip and overturning the tables – but it actually appears to have involved no actual physical harming of people. If it had done then there would surely have been willing witnesses to come forward at his trial just a few days later. His words about 'destroying the Temple' are cited against him during the trial, but no one can be found to supply evidence of guilt.

So symbolic, prophetic action is, sometimes, justified in our pursuit of justice. Good examples would include the massive peaceful protest in Edinburgh for Make Poverty History with which this book began, or the quiet sit-down protests in front of the arms fair held in East London. But when protests turn to violence, including verbal violence, they start falling into the trap of resorting to the very falsehoods they are seeking to stop or change.

We live in a violent world. Sadly child abuse of all kinds is rife across the planet; domestic violence affects huge numbers of women (and some men); violent crime damages people of all ages; racially motivated violence feeds further racial prejudice and division; war scars nations and peoples; and verbal violence fuels it all at every level. We are all tempted to join in at some level or another. We need to learn from Jesus the wisdom of silence, the fruitlessness of retaliation, the ultimate impotence of violence and the power of peace.

Ideas for reflection

1 In what ways have you been a victim of violence? Have you ever shared this with anyone else? With God? Is it time to do so now?
2 In what ways does the temptation to resort to violence come to you? What mechanisms do you have for resisting this? Does diversion work?
3 Are you aware of someone who is the victim of violence? In what ways might you be able to support them?

Pictures

Jesus Mafa: *The Whipping*
Dinah Roe Kendall: *The Crucifixion*
Sidney Spencer: *The Eagles*

Prayer

Prince of Peace, we cry to you for the victims of violence;
for their healing and wholeness.
Prince of Peace, we cry to you for the perpetrators of violence;
for their judgement and forgiveness;
for their change of heart and mind.
Prince of Peace, we cry to you for ourselves as victims and
    perpetrators;
for your compassion and transformation of our lives. Amen.

10

Sex: licence and fidelity

British society appears to be obsessed with sex. The biggest selling newspapers are filled every day with stories of the alleged sexual exploits of pop singers, footballers and the stars of stage and screen. The TV soaps are full of relationships and affairs. TV and radio comedy shows are filled with both explicit and implicit sexual references. TV chat shows are often focussed around sexual innuendo. A growing percentage of 'children's' TV has sexual references and activities. I dread to think how much sexual activity and reference the average TV viewer is exposed to in a week. A very large percentage of this will be casual and extramarital activity; some of it will be of a same-sex nature; increasingly references are made to under-age sex, sex with minors and bestiality as 'okay' for some. Very little of what is broadcast or published will be about happily, faithfully married couples enjoying a fulfilling intimate relationship (though some will be).

The very exposure to this means that sexual temptation will happen to virtually everyone. However, I do not want to suggest that this is all the media's fault or simply a modern phenomenon. The media would not keep producing what they do if it did not sell newspapers, raise viewing figures and attract advertising revenue. The buying, watching and listening public has to take responsibility for its own choices. Then literature and history tell us that sexual promiscuity has been a feature of societies and cultures right down through history; a quick reading of the history of the Greek and Roman Empires reveals this. We are sexual beings and as such can choose either to use our sexuality for the glory of God or merely for our own gratification. We can make an idol of sex; we can also rejoice in it as a God-given gift.

A Russian tale

The story that follows happened on my second visit to Russia for Scripture Union. The first trip had been something of a nightmare. Communism was just breaking down and Mikhail Gorbachev was starting to introduce reforms. I queued for an hour in a supermarket with my Russian host for a few potatoes, some onions and cabbage. There was nothing else on the shelves to buy. After a few days it became clear that my visit had been badly planned by my host and I found myself with no work to do. I had the answer I had been sent for; this person was not suitable to be the key person with whom to begin Scripture Union work in post-communist Moscow. But to discover this answer I had experienced extreme loneliness and massive frustration, and I had seriously thought that I would never return to Russia again. Now I had been persuaded that this second trip would be better.

The first few days in St Petersburg were a huge improvement. It was a wonderful city to be in for a few days (even before all the massive investment that has subsequently taken place). My hosts were much friendlier, more organized and were those with whom it appeared that Scripture Union could work. But they were, understandably, reserved and cautious. Communication with home was almost impossible. Loneliness began to return. I then travelled alone, overnight, to Moscow on the train. On my arrival no one was there to meet me. I eventually found my way to my new Muscovite hosts by taxi (and was decidedly ripped off by the driver). They were unapologetic for the error that had left me uncollected. Over the next 48 hours it became abundantly clear that yet again I was being hosted by people who were far from suitable partners for Scripture Union.

The loneliness became more intense than anything I had ever experienced. I found myself assailed by sexual fantasies and desires that I had never known before. The longings were intense and the fantasies weird. All I longed for was some human warmth and touch. I realized that I had had almost no physical contact of any form (not even a handshake) for several days. For the first time in my life I understood why some businessmen turn to prostitutes when away from home. There is a longing for contact. There can be a level of frustration that it is perceived can be relieved by engagement with one working in the 'sex trade'. Somehow I prayed in the midst of the fantasies. Eventually they subsided; and I fell asleep, I think, through the exhaustion of the inner battles that took place. I could not believe that I could feel or think quite this way. I felt deeply guilty that here I was as an emissary for a great Christian organization in a pioneering role yet thinking such thoughts. I felt guilty towards Rosemary for my mental infidelity. It was not easy to tell her about it when I returned home, but tell her, eventually, I did.

Changing attitudes

I have lived faithfully and very happily with Rosemary for the 24 years of our marriage. We have been blessed with four fabulous children. Before we met I had had a number of girlfriends through my teenage years and early twenties. Some were casual relationships (though they often felt intense at the time, that is after all the way of many teenage relationships); some more serious and long-lasting. The level of kissing, cuddling and so on varied from one relationship to another. The older I became the more precious I realized every aspect of physical intimacy actually is, and the more respect I understood should be shown to the partner. I was not what would be regarded as promiscuous or even widely sexually experienced. But, at the risk of sounding like a prudish middle-aged man, I wish I had been even more thoughtful and cautious than I was. Exploring intimacy with one partner for life is, I believe, the richest and fullest sexual experience available to us all.

The temptation to think and act otherwise will, however, always be with us.

Sadly, though not surprisingly, I have known a number of Christians, some in leadership roles, who have succumbed to sexual temptation. Sexual intercourse before marriage, adultery, paedophilia, sadomasochism and self-abuse have all featured in pastoral conversations over the years. In recent years the growth of indulging sexual fantasies through pictures and video clips on the Internet has become a major concern. It is largely men who are guilty of this, though there is also a disturbing growth among women. Pornographic magazines have been around for a long time; these have fuelled men's fantasies. Some of these have become more graphic. However, the Internet has created a whole new level of explicit imagery. This is disturbing not simply for the men and women who look at the images but for the people who have often been abused in order that the images are created in the first place.

People indulge in such fantasies for a whole range of reasons; their own loneliness, their deep inner unhappiness, their sense of inadequacy, their failed relationships and their sheer desire for ever more graphic images and experiences are all contributory factors.

The simplest solution to offer is to avoid all of this; simply do not get started. However, for those who have already indulged in such fantasies, breaking away from it is not as simple as saying, 'Stop'. Almost certainly some will not find the strength to resist the temptation without being honest about the problem with others, and enlisting their encouragement and support through prayer to help them have the will to stop. A married man may need the support of another man or two. He will also need the courage to be honest with his wife about the problem. Single persons who find themselves indulging in this partly through their loneliness and frustrations will often need the strong support of good friends. In some cases there will certainly be a need for counselling to tackle the underlying issues of loneliness, inadequacy or having been abused themselves. Very few who become deeply involved in the use of the Internet for sexual fantasy appear to be able to stop without the help and support of others.

In a society which has become rather obsessed with sex it is not surprising that sexual temptation is common. The reality is that in one form or another sexual temptation has been high on the list throughout all of human history and exists in every culture and society.

Jesus and sexual temptation

So did Jesus face such temptations? If he did then what help does he offer us in seeking to live lives of fidelity today?

Earlier in this book, when considering how Jesus was tempted all his life, we noted that he experienced puberty, as is common to almost everyone. In puberty he would have faced the same temptations, set within his own culture, that all pubescents face.

As he went into early adulthood he no doubt faced questions about when he would marry. It was the cultural norm that everyone should marry. Marriages were generally 'arranged' by the parents. So somewhere along the line Jesus must have had conversations with Mary and Joseph about his future. They were aware of cousin John, son of Zechariah and Elizabeth, being raised as a Nazirite, which would mean that he would probably not marry. I think we can safely assume that, in their conversations, Jesus, Mary and Joseph would have discussed what it might mean for Jesus to work out his calling as God's Anointed One. Probably together they concluded that this meant remaining single. Such a decision would have brought surprise to Jesus' fellow Nazarenes. They may well have asked many questions about why Jesus did not marry. There surely must have been plenty of parents with daughters who would have loved to see one of them married to the carpenter who was held in such favour by the local community.

When later Jesus was teaching his disciples about marriage and divorce he spoke these words: 'For there are eunuchs who have been so from birth, and there are eunuchs who have been made eunuchs by others, and there are eunuchs who have made themselves eunuchs for the sake of the kingdom of heaven' (Matthew 19.12). It seems most likely that this latter phrase is Jesus' own self-description. He had deliberately chosen a life of celibacy for the sake of God's kingdom.

Yet this was put to the test during his ministry.

The women and Jesus

In Simon the Pharisee's house, while at a meal, a woman comes in and anoints Jesus' feet with oil, weeps over his feet and dries the tears with her hair. Everyone present it seems knew enough about this woman to refer to her as a 'sinner' (Luke 7.36–39). This may well mean she was a prostitute. The act she undertakes is potentially filled with sexual energy both for herself and for Jesus. Her act is one of love for the one who has forgiven her but everyone present recognized its 'immoral' potential as well – that is why they are amazed that Jesus does not stop her. Yet there is no hint, even from his detractors, of moral failure on Jesus' part. The sexual temptation was surely there but he chose to reject it.

Jesus travelled around Israel not only with his 12 disciples but also with other men and women (Luke 8.1–3). Some of these women's backgrounds were at best disreputable. Mary Magdalene had been in bondage to evil spirits before Jesus released her and she became one of his leading followers (Luke 8.2). The myth that she was in fact secretly married to Jesus has been popularized again in recent times by Dan Brown's *Da Vinci Code*. Tim Rice and Andrew Lloyd Webber's musical *Jesus Christ Superstar* also hints at a sexual attraction between Mary and Jesus. While neither has solid basis in the gospel accounts, the idea that at least one of the women in Jesus' company was attracted to him sexually is not at all unreasonable. Neither is it unreasonable to believe that Jesus was himself physically and sexually attracted to at least one of the women. However, he knew what he meant when he was teaching about choosing celibacy for the sake of the kingdom of God. In whatever ways he was tempted by sexual attraction he chose not to accept it.

Jesus and the disciple whom he loved

Some have also posed the possibility of Jesus being of homosexual orientation. The references to 'the beloved disciple', traditionally identified as John the apostle (John 13.23; 19.26; 20.2; 21.7, 20) have been taken to indicate not simply a particularly close relationship between Jesus and the disciple but an active homosexual one. Now this idea falls into the trap of interpretation through our own culture's oversexualized eyes. We seem to have reached the point where we cannot accept that a relationship between two men can be very deep but not involve sexual expression. Indeed we are at the same point when it comes to relationships between a man and a woman. Yet such deep relationships are not only possible; they are to be valued, encouraged and developed. Men need deep relationships with other men; women need deep relationships with other women; a man and a woman can have a very deep relationship without it involving sexual activity.

Yet those who wish to offer this homosexual interpretation (as they do also of that between David and Jonathan (1 Samuel 20; 2 Samuel 1.26) have highlighted the fact that Jesus might well have faced the temptation to indulge in homosexual activity. He was fully man. He faced the same temptations that we do. So this temptation cannot be excluded from him. Yet again we have to note that he chose the way of celibacy for the sake of the kingdom of God.

Jesus and marriage

In his teaching Jesus clearly endorsed marriage, between one man and one woman for life, as God's gift in creation (Matthew 19.4–6). It was in this relationship that Jesus endorsed sexual activity, for he pronounced adultery as sinful on a number of occasions (Matthew 5.27–30; 19.9; Mark 7.21). His cousin and forerunner John the Baptist had also preached about purity in marriage, and found himself first imprisoned and then beheaded for challenging Herod on this point. Jesus always endorsed John and his ministry. We can assume he concurred with John's assessment of Herod and Herodias' marriage.

While being very clear on the God-given goodness and uniqueness of marriage and the sinfulness of adultery Jesus also made it clear that forgiveness was available. He gave forgiveness and a whole fresh start to those who had fallen into sexual sin (Luke 7.47; John 4.15–42; 8.1–11) but his expectation was of wholesome sexual living from then on (John 8.11).

So we discover from Jesus that he did face sexual temptation, just as we do. Jesus was fully human and was therefore sexually aware. He must, I have suggested, have experienced sexual temptation. Since he was not married, sexual involvement of any kind would have been regarded by him and his contemporaries as outside God's best for his people. So he must have chosen to resist the temptations that came his way.

We live in a culture which has raised sex and sexuality to an extraordinary status. We are bombarded by it. My experience is that I have, sadly, known a number of ministers whose ministry has been either ruined or deeply damaged through giving in to the temptation to sexual infidelity. I have wept with families destroyed through a husband's, a wife's or a child's decision to give in to such temptations. I have also seen the grace of God rebuilding people's lives – for sexual infidelity is no less redeemable and forgivable than any other sin. So how do we resist sexual temptation? Often the simplest answer is to avoid it. Watch less TV that is sexually explicit. Avoid reading newspapers and literature that overstimulate. Avoid being alone with someone whom you find sexually attractive. Sometimes, for work reasons, this may be unavoidable. Then ensure that you sit sensibly apart. Don't work too long or too late; tiredness weakens our defences, so does alcohol.

But it appears that the key factor lies in knowing and understanding what God wants of us in serving his kingdom. If he wants us to be single for the sake of his kingdom's business then that conviction is what will hold us fast to living God's way of celibacy. It is quite simply a lie that we have to have sexual experience to live a full life. Jesus lived the fullest, most wonderful life ever lived and he did so as a celibate.

For those of us called to marriage (for it is a calling and a gift from God – 1 Corinthians 7.7), lifelong faithfulness is our commitment. This will not always be easy. As the years go by each of us will change, children may enter the family and so the relationship must adapt and grow. Developing intimacy with one another at every level is essential. Temptation to settle for less than the best may come. Temptation to look for excitement with someone else does develop for many. But holding on to the vows made before God at the outset remains the basis on which to resist such temptations.

The best piece of advice I was given here was several years ago by a good older friend who was also one to whom I looked as a mentor. His marriage had come to an end. Rosemary and I asked him, 'What's to stop us being in the same position as you are now in 20 years' time?' His reply was simple – 'Never say or think, "It could never happen to us".' Every married couple has to be alert to the possibility of being tempted to infidelity.

But fidelity to God's ways will lead to the most satisfying life. For some this is fidelity to singleness; for others it is fidelity to marriage. In a world that has become oversexualized and finds it apparently impossible to think that such single-mindedness is either possible or desirable, upholding such lives will never be easy, but it will be worth it.

Ideas for reflection

1 Be honest with yourself about your own sexual temptations. Do you need to take any action in relation to what you read, watch on TV, or look at on the Internet?

2 Take time to reflect on Jesus' handling of his relationships with women and men.
3 Bring your sexuality and sexual desires before God.

Pictures

Jesus Mafa: *Cana Wedding* and *Samaritan Woman* or *Penitent Woman*
Dinah Roe Kendall: *Woman Taken in Adultery*

Prayer

Creator God, thank you for making human beings as male and female. Thank you for our complementarity and our sexuality. Praise you for the goodness of sexual expression within marriage.

Help me to live with my own sexuality in holiness. Amen.

11

Legalism and grace

I was with my beloved friends and colleagues, the clergy of Byumba Diocese, Rwanda. These women and men are an inspiring group. Every one of them has been through more trauma than I have. Every single one of them has lost family members through war, genocide or HIV/AIDS. Most have lost more than one person in such a way. Many have experienced having to leave their home in fear of their lives. They have lived in displaced persons and refugee camps. They have known hunger, thirst, pain and sickness beyond anything I have experienced. They handle deep poverty every day of their lives. Yet they smile and laugh; they enjoy life; they remain faithful to the good news of God in Jesus Christ. It has been my privilege to share with them in one way or another every year for the past nine years. They have taught me so much about following Christ.

Yet on this occasion I was becoming increasingly frustrated with them. The discussion was amazingly similar to many I have had with clergy in Britain. Questions about funerals, marriages, baptisms and Communion were all under discussion. My frustration was growing because of the apparent longing from many to be able to offer nice neat packaged answers to every last situation that arises. They wanted a rule to cover every circumstance. Part of the desire was fine; they wanted to ensure that services were conducted well and appropriately to the occasion. But sometimes creeping into the discussion there came more than a hint of

wanting to ensure that the Church was kept 'pure' by only allowing the 'right' people to participate. Anyone watching would have
seen the huge physical sigh of relief that coursed through my body
as Elson arose and spoke of the need for grace and not law to
govern how we handle people and situations. He spoke clearly,
eloquently, and above all graciously as he rebuked his colleagues
for having become tied up in legal knots about godparents, fu-
neral rites and communion stewards, rather than being governed
by grace. The even greater relief came as everyone acknowledged
the wisdom and correctness of his words. The session closed with
a commitment by all to ensure that they ran all such services
well, and that this meant grace and graciousness must be at
their heart.

Let me turn to a rather trivial example from the writing of this
book. 'Spider Solitaire' on the computer can be both a blessing and
a curse. There are times when the mind needs a break from writing; it needs to function differently. Sometimes a walk around the
garden has been called for; but at times SS has worked well as a
refreshing break. At other times it has simply been a distraction,
wasting valuable time and makes me wish it was not on the computer at all. Now the temptation towards wanting rules for everything leads to someone asking the question, 'Is playing Spider
Solitaire a good or a bad activity?' or perhaps to nuance it a little
more, 'When is it okay to play SS and when is it wrong to do so?'
The legal mind wants a clearly defined answer to the question;
it struggles with fuzzy edges. This is a very trivial illustration,
especially in view of the hard questions my Rwandan friends were
discussing, but I hope it makes the point. It does perhaps point
up that sometimes we become overconcerned about the trivial
rather than the heart of matters. That was certainly true of some
of the Rwandan discussions; lots of heat about the right way to
exchange the rings during a wedding service, and little about the
purpose of marriage! We all suffer from a constant temptation
towards legalism.

Pharisees rule OK?

Jesus' continual three-year struggle with the scribes and the Pharisees centred round legalism. The Pharisees were passionate for wanting to do the right thing. They wanted to please God; to live by his laws. But this was where Jesus became so enraged with them. They saw it all as human effort, as doing the right thing all the time, rather than as a greater matter of justice and grace. All of Jesus' harshest words were reserved for the religious leaders of his day. They were on occasions very harsh; 'Woe to you scribes and Pharisees, hypocrites . . . woe to you blind guides.' He calls them 'blind guides, whitewashed tombs and snakes, a brood of vipers' (Matthew 23.16, 27, 33). Such strong words understandably did not endear Jesus to them at all. His complaint, his judgement on them, was that they had become so caught up with defining the details of the law that they had lost sight of the big issues of justice, mercy and faith. He saw them as those who were continually trying to burden others with petty rules while failing to live by example. He saw them ultimately as those who kept people away from God rather than bringing them into God's grace and presence.

It is very easy to join in the criticism of the Pharisees. We forget just how radical Jesus was being in criticizing them. These were the religious leaders, the ones who studied the law and taught it; these were the people to whom everyone looked for guidance. I have to continually remind myself that as a religious leader today I might be rather closer to the Pharisees than I care to admit. How very easily, when people seek advice, I fall into the trap of offering specific guidelines. How quickly church guidelines designed for good idea and practice turn into rigid rules. How smoothly we slide into legally binding people up rather than offering them freedom.

Grace has always been God's way of working with human beings. He first rescued and delivered Israel from their Egyptian bondage before he gave them the Ten Commandments and the law. The commandments came as response to God's saving grace not as the means of earning it. The whole sacrificial system emphasized the need for grace and forgiveness because we all make mistakes. The law taught generosity to others, mirroring God's generosity to the people. Grace has to come first because by the way of law there is no hope for any human being. The law succeeds only in pointing up our weaknesses, our failures and our sins; it can never provide us with a way of salvation and forgiveness. For this we are dependent on mercy and grace.

The Pharisees had fallen foul of believing that they could earn God's favour through meticulous detailed observation of the law. Jesus knew that this led only to bondage and hopelessness. Hope lay in the breaking-in of God's mercy and love. Hope lay in a Father who welcomes home the errant son; a Shepherd who would do anything to rescue the lost sheep; a Creator who provides; a God who loves so much that he gives his one and only Son.

Grace and lawlessness

The apostle Paul taught grace so much that he was at times accused of not only denigrating the law but encouraging lawlessness. He tackles the accusation with his usual vigour in his letter to the Romans (especially chapter 6). It is a debate that has continued ever since. Grace is about acceptance, welcome, forgiveness. In grace God puts us right with himself through Jesus' death on the cross. Like the father in the parable, he runs to welcome us home, throws his arms around us dirty as we are, and places the ring of sonship or daughterhood on our finger. It is all grace; undeserved, overwhelming, amazing.

So if he loves us this much and forgives us, why not sin again and again simply so that we can receive more grace? It does not hold water as an argument. How can the blind whose sight has been restored go out and blind themselves again just to have another experience of being made to see again? How can the lame person made to walk go out deliberately and break a leg just to experience a new leg again? It makes no sense. When a woman who was blind is given her sight back, she lives in thankfulness for the gift; she uses her eyes, she does not abuse them. Ask anyone in Uganda whose sight has been restored by a simple cataract operation and he will tell you how wonderful it is to see again and how ridiculous it would be to destroy that sight. When a man who could not walk has his leg restored he lives in thankfulness for his new mobility; he uses his leg well, he does not abuse it. Ask anyone who has discovered the joy of freedom from pain and the liberty to walk well again after a hip replacement.

When one has experienced the glorious freedom of total forgiveness by God and the loving acceptance of the Father it is unthinkable to live in anything other than thankfulness for grace. Life has to be given in service of the One who is love.

Yet the temptation to lawlessness comes. The sneaking thought, 'Well, it does not matter if I go against God just this one time, after all he'll forgive me,' creeps into our minds. 'Just this once', however, can easily develop into a habit. The alcoholic knows that once off the booze he has to stay off; 'just one drink' does not work for an addict. 'Just one sin' does not work for us either; we cannot presume on God's grace; we cannot throw it back in his face. Although in fact we do, time and time and time again. Yet in grace he goes on holding us, cleansing us and renewing us. Our only hope lies in staying in this grace.

The attraction of legalism

So when grace is so wonderful why do we become distracted by legalism? The attraction lies, often, in our ability to control, to manipulate and to decide for ourselves. Determining the tithing of dill, cumin and mint for the Pharisees allowed them to control the situation; and to exercise control over others. It also allowed them to ignore the weightier matters of justice for the poor and mercy for the sinner.

It has regularly stunned me in church council meetings how a group of mature adults can spend ages arguing about the arrangement of the chairs, or the cost of the after-service coffee, but then happily decide to spend several thousand pounds on a project with almost no discussion. When now, as a bishop, I visit church councils I am amazed by the regularity with which I will be asked about matters which are really ones of detail, and how easily major issues which confront the church at local, national and international levels are left to one side. It is easier to handle the small and the local; this we can control, or at least try to do so. If we can find ways of creating regulations that enable us to exercise some control over others we will do so. This is the attraction; clarity, security and control.

Grace on the other hand is messy, very messy. Grace is about guilty thieves being forgiven with their dying breath; grace is about child abusers discovering a freedom from their past; grace is about the perpetrators of genocide discovering forgiveness. Grace is about extraordinary generosity. It is risky. Grace struggles to define the edges tightly; it worries little about the things which ultimately do not matter; it is concerned only with the weightiest things of the universe – death, life, failure, forgiveness, justice, freedom.

Legalism is attractive because we can get our heads around it; it offers us control. Grace is outside our grasp and control; grace says we are dependent on another for hope and for life. Grace trains us 'to renounce impiety and worldly passions, and in the present age to live lives that are self-controlled, upright, and godly, while we wait for the blessed hope and the manifestation of the glory of our great God and Saviour, Jesus Christ' (Titus 2.12–13).

Ideas for reflection

1 Are there particular 'laws' that you judge yourself and others by?
2 Read the story of the 'lost son' and the 'running father' and 'angry brother' in Luke 15.11–32. In what ways are you like the lost son? In what ways like the angry elder brother? How do you experience God as like this father?

3 In what ways is grace messy and risky? How might this show itself in your and your church's life?

Pictures

Jesus Mafa: *Prodigal Son*
Sidney Spencer: *The Hen*
Dinah Roe Kendall: *Mary Anoints Jesus' Feet*

Prayer

Blessed be you, God and Father of our Lord Jesus Christ,

For you have blessed us in Christ with every spiritual blessing in the heavenly places;

You chose us in Christ before the foundation of the world to be holy and blameless before him in love.

You destined us for adoption as your children through Jesus Christ according to the good pleasure of your will.

Praise to your glorious grace which you have freely bestowed on us in your Beloved in whom we have redemption through his blood, the forgiveness of our trespasses,

according to the riches of your grace which you have lavished upon us.

Hallelujah!

(Based on Ephesians 1.3–8)

12

Doubt and certainty

The simple truth is that I cannot remember ever doubting God's existence until after I became a committed Christian as a teen-ager. Since then there have been both fleeting points and longer periods of such doubt. Sometimes the doubt is not about God's existence, but it is about what God is like; does he really care about this world or me? I have certainly wrestled with doubts about my own calling to full-time ministry and my current ministry as a bishop. Doubt has been, and remains, part of my Christian experience.

Then there have been the times of certainty. I have been cer-tain of the right, or wrong, thing to do. I have been certain of God's call and direction. Sometimes that certainty has proved to be well founded; but on other occasions I have been proved quite wrong in my own certainty. This has led, variously, to embarrassment, confusion, questioning and doubt. Doubt and certainty seem to be very close companions at times.

Doubt strikes

Around 20 teenagers piled out of the McKays' house. It had been a good evening; the usual mix of laughter, gentle kind banter, singing and serious conversation about being a disciple of Jesus. Outside in the road a friendly argument broke out between my sister Mary and her best friend Joyce. Joyce had jumped on to the back of Jim's Honda 50. Mary thought that she was due to travel back to Chessington with Jim. Joyce won the day. Mary climbed into a car and set off; soon after Jim followed, with Joyce holding on tightly. I was on my bike. I watched Jim turn the corner and go out of sight. After a few words with those still left I also set off. As I rounded the bend of the main road a horrible sight awaited me. There lying in the road, having run straight into the back of an unlit skip, were Jim and Joyce. Moments later a car, filled with friends, pulled up; this was the early 1970s so there were no mobile phones to hand. An ambulance was called by a local resident. There was nothing any of us could do other than try and make them both comfortable and wait; both were unconscious. In a matter of seconds the lives of all of us had been changed. Jim and Joyce both died from their injuries. He was 17, she was 14. They were wonderful people, full of life, and with, we all thought, bright futures.

Such an event shakes families, communities and individuals. The number of times the question 'Why?' was asked was innumerable. Together we supported one another in the youth group and church. Our families were all hugely supportive as well. Innocent, blameless loss of life like this inevitably makes one doubt God's activity and purposes; even his reality. It certainly made me doubt all kinds of things about the faith in which I was still very young. To this day there are occasions where I find tears welling up in my eyes for my two friends, and their families. I still cannot offer a full answer to the question 'Why?' I do know, however, that this shaped my life in many ways. It made me acutely aware of the brevity of life. It caused me to realize that none of us knows how long we have left to live. It has, through the years, acted as an imperative for me to serve God as fully as I can while I can, leaving in his hands exactly how long I might have left to live. I know it has shaped the lives of all of us who knew them well.

Suffering, especially the suffering of the innocent, has probably caused me to ask more questions than anything else in my life. The hunger and poverty I have seen in many parts of Africa; the suffering of those living with HIV/AIDS; or the traumatic losses of those living in a refugee or displaced persons camp have all made me wonder deeply about life making any sense at all. It is impossible, I find, not to sit with people in such circumstances and cry out, 'Lord, why?' 'Lord, how long before there is justice for the poor?' 'Where are you in all this?'

There are no straightforward and clear answers to the questions, although I have become ever more aware that so much suffering is caused by humankind's own fault. Our comfortable consumer lifestyle is at the expense of others. I am complicit in creating the suffering of the hungry and the homeless because of the unjust ways in which we treat people and nations and establish trade rules. It is wrong to blame God for that which is our fault as people who have failed to exercise our 'dominion' over creation fairly or carefully. In the case of Jim and Joyce someone had put a skip on a blind bend, and had failed to ensure it was lit. Someone's stupidity led to the deaths of two young people.

Yet while there are no straightforward answers I have discovered that the suffering of God as a human being makes more sense of it all than anything else. God is not distant from our suffering; he has entered into it and experienced it. The suffering of Christ on the cross is the suffering of God with us, and for us. It does not give me an answer to every last detailed question, in every last circumstance, but it does tell me God cares and is not distant from our suffering at all. Indeed rather he is in the midst of it all with us. The presence and reality of God is, it seems, to be found more profoundly with the suffering than with those living at ease and in comfort.

The Scriptures are full of people with doubts. They are filled with people asking the very same questions about 'Why?' and 'How long?' that we have. The book of Job, Ecclesiastes and many of the Psalms are filled with searching about such questions. So too the prophets find themselves wondering what God is doing among his people and the nations.

But my own doubts are expressed in other ways. Does God really love me? I can see why he should love others, but is it true for me? I can look at other Christians; their prayers seem to be answered more often and more dramatically than mine. They seem to experience God's Spirit more powerfully than I do. God just seems more real to them and closer to them than to me. Perhaps God doesn't really value me as much. Such doubts continue to arise at times. They have never gone away completely.

These doubts I find answered through the words of Scripture describing all Christians, not just a few. Passages like those in Ephesians 1, Colossians 1, 1 Peter 1 and 1 John 3 all speak profoundly of God's amazing love for us all. I find these doubts also respond to remembering that I have been baptized. It was Martin Luther who, when assailed by doubts about his salvation, is said to have thrown his ink pot at the devil crying, 'I am baptized.' In baptism we are bound into Christ. It is the sacrament of initiation not simply where we identify ourselves with Christ but where he identifies himself with us. Remembering our baptism is important in times of doubt.

So too is Holy Communion. Receiving the bread and wine we remember all that God has done for us in the death of Jesus. Yet as we remember so God meets with us in this simple meal. It acts as a point of renewal so that we are freshly empowered and enriched to serve Christ in the world. Communion takes us back to the heart of the suffering God.

Doubt, then, is common to us all. Different kinds of doubt affect us. But facing the doubt, and pursuing the questions, can strengthen us and deepen us in our faith. Doubt is not to be seen as a terrible enemy; it can be seen as an opportunity to grow and deepen our understanding of God and his ways.

Jesus and doubt

This is one way of seeing what was happening with Jesus in the wilderness. He is tempted to and by doubt. 'If you are the Son of God' is the opening of two of the temptations. Satan appears to be saying to Jesus, 'So you heard a voice, did you? Declaring you the beloved Son of the Almighty – are you sure that's the truth? Is that who you really are?' Then the temptations follow to act in a way to prove or demonstrate such sonship. Jesus was tempted therefore to doubt his identity and to doubt the Father's word to him. What happens, though, is not simply a rebuttal of the doubt; it is also a deepening of Jesus' grasp on both his identity and his calling. Somehow he returns from the wilderness with clarity about how he should conduct his ministry and live as the Beloved Son. Doubt turns into deeper understanding through reflection on the Scriptures, the creation around him, his life thus far and prayer. The temptation thus turns into growth; doubt becomes not a stone on which to fall but a rock on which to build.

In this sense Jesus returned from the wilderness with a certainty about how he should conduct his ministry that had perhaps not been there before he entered it. As his ministry unfolded over the following three years there appeared to be a clarity, a certainty about him. From the time of Peter's great confession Jesus taught his disciples that he, the Son of Man, 'must' suffer and die (Matthew 16.21; Mark 10.33–34; Luke 17.25). After his resurrection this is the theme of his teaching to the disciples. He explains from the Scriptures why he 'had to' suffer and die (Luke 24.25–27, 44–49).

Jesus and certainty

So there was a certainty about Jesus in knowing his identity and calling. He was certain that he had to go to the cross. Yet this certainty was born out of hard testing; it came out of lifelong reflection and it was tested deeply time and again with the temptation to choose a different way.

There are times too where Jesus is seen to challenge certainty. The Pharisees were certain about their understanding of the law, and of how salvation could be earned through total obedience to it. Jesus challenged them in their certainty about their rightness on many occasions (Mark 2.23—3.6). The Sadducees were equally certain that they were correct about the stupidity of believing in angels or the resurrection. Jesus challenged them about their certainty, and left them disturbed by his answers (Luke 20.27–38).

He even had to challenge the disciples about their certainty when they were sure that they were right to stop one ministering in Jesus' name because they were not part of the disciples' band (Luke 9.49–50). Certainty, it appears, is not always the best position in which to be. It can blind us to different possibilities. It can limit us.

There is a great attraction in certainty. It makes us feel safe and secure. In a world of rapid change in which our moorings seem to have become lost then certainty has a huge appeal. It is one of the reasons why there has been a growth in religious 'fundamentalism' of all kinds in many different societies and cultures. But certainty can tempt us into rigidity. It can lead us to always play safe, refusing to take the risks of change and growth. This is part of the falsehood into which the religious leaders of Jesus' day appeared to have fallen. They had fixed ideas about how the law was to be interpreted. They also had fixed ideas about what God's Messiah would be like. When the Messiah turned out to be a suffering servant their certainty meant that they could not see the reality. The temptation has remained ever since; all of us are in the constant danger of locking God into a box; of fixing with certainty the God who is always surprising.

Now this is not to say that there is no place for confidence or assurance in our faith. The inner witness of God's Holy Spirit assuring us that we are God's children and that Jesus died and rose for us is real. I have my times of doubt but I am also sure that God loves me and has called me into his family. I know God is real. But this inner assurance comes from faith, not provable certainties. If I relied on provable evidence then there is plenty which seems contrary – the suffering I have already mentioned; but there is also the mystery of why one person is healed and another is not; of why unjust corrupt rulers remain in power when God promises to bring them down. There is the way in which the Church is persecuted and sidelined; and its lack of unity when the one thing for which Jesus prayed for the Church was unity. St Paul was making this point to the Corinthians when he wrote, 'for we walk by faith, not by sight' (2 Corinthians 5.7). His circumstances seemed quite contrary to the idea that in Christ God had dealt with sin and injustice; they certainly seemed contrary to the notion that Paul was an apostle, as suffering was his regular experience. Yet he writes, 'So we are always confident'; he knew God was in control; he knew God was upholding him. He knew it because of the cross of Christ: 'For the love of Christ urges us on, because we are convinced that one has died for all; therefore all have died' (2 Corinthians 5.14).

So confidence in God is possible. Assurance that God's love is in control and that his purposes will work out is a real Christian experience. This comes as the inner witness of the Spirit, rooted in the death and resurrection of Jesus. It is different from certainty in ourselves and our own abilities; it can never be arrogant or overbearing because it rests in God himself. As the writer to the Hebrews puts it, 'faith is the assurance of things hoped for, the conviction of things not seen' (Hebrews 11.1).

This was how Jesus dealt with doubt and certainty in Gethsemane. He was sure that he must go through suffering; yet he wondered if there was another possible way. He was confident that his Father would vindicate him and raise him from the dead but there was only one way for that to happen: to go to the cross and die. He lived with an assurance of things hoped for and a conviction of things not seen – but it was painful, costly, tough and risky.

In following Christ, doubts will come; with them will come the temptations to stop believing and give up. In following Christ, assurance will be there but so too will the temptation to turn this into solid certainties rather than a life of faith and adventure. Doubts can be the stepping stones into deeper understandings but these will always need to be held in faith. Thomas has been permanently saddled with the title 'doubter' because he wanted the certainty of seeing and touching Christ's wounds. Jesus gave him what he wanted but also promised, 'Blessed are those who have not seen and yet have come to believe' (John 20.24–29).

Ideas for reflection

1 What causes you to doubt? How do you handle this?
2 What dangers are there for you in doubt?
3 What dangers are there in certainty?
4 In what ways might God be calling you at present to 'walk by faith and not by sight'?

Pictures

Jesus Mafa: *Jesus and Thomas*
Sidney Spencer: *He Departed into a Mountain to Pray*
Dinah Roe Kendall: *When the Sword Pierced Her Own Soul*

Prayer

Lord, I believe, help my unbelief.

Lord, I like certainties. I like to be sure, to know exactly what is happening; what is expected. I like firm ground. Teach me to trust you; teach me to walk by faith, to step into the uncertain assured that you are already there. Amen.

13

Blame and forgiveness

The opening session of the conference had gone really well. The worship band had played and sung superbly; all those reading and leading prayers had done so excellently. The speaker had made a first-class address. There was an enormously positive feel among the 500 delegates present. So, having had a key role in planning it all, and having led the session I was feeling pretty good. Then over coffee someone whom I value and respect approached me; 'Paul, I'm sorry but I feel very upset. One hymn we sang jarred deeply – it was its lack of inclusive language that hurt. I'm afraid I couldn't settle for the rest of the session.' I was stunned. Immediately I went into defensive mode. It wasn't my fault; the band had chosen the song and supplied the lyrics. Graciously my upset friend took this and apologized for blaming me. I soon realized what I had done. I was, after all, in overall responsibility for the session. I knew I had changed the lyrics for a hymn to be used later in the day to ensure that they were inclusive. I should have spotted what was actually a glaring point. I confess it took me several days before I sent an honest and apologetic e-mail accepting responsibility rather than deflecting it on to others. I had to resist putting in all kinds of caveats and reasons to diminish my own responsibility; for this is what I, and we, always seem to do.

The blame game

We like to shift the blame on to someone, or something else (such as circumstances). We try and diminish our own responsibility rather than accepting our mistakes, and our sins.

We hear government ministers answering questions in Parliament shifting the blame on to others rather than accepting their own responsibility. Children at school will seek to point the finger at the child sitting next to them: 'It was him, Miss, not me.' A driver will seek to avoid accepting responsibility for an accident by pointing the finger of blame at the other driver, or an incident on the other carriageway, or a pedestrian, rather than taking the blame themselves. Sometimes people seek to place the blame on their upbringing, or the environment in which they live and work. Certainly our upbringing shapes us greatly; a child who is not loved will find it hard to love. Someone who is abused as a child we know is more likely to become a child abuser themselves – but not all do. Some choose not to repeat the pattern. A proper recognition of the factors in our childhood experiences which shape the way we feel, think and behave is certainly right; this may lead to recognition of reduced responsibility on occasions. However, to go through life blaming the past, or even the present environment, is to fail to take responsibility for our own lives and decisions. We can blame others all we like but each of us makes decisions about how we will respond to those events and situations. Each of us can choose to respond differently. We can break out from the bonds of the past.

I was visiting a high-rise block of flats. Within the same block I visited flats that were immaculately kept and beautifully decorated, and those that were absolutely squalid. On some floors the landings were clean, tidy and smart; on others they stank of urine and vomit and were covered in graffiti. The basic environment was the same for all; the people chose to respond to and use the environment differently. Blame for the unwholesome parts of the block lay with human choices and actions, not the environment.

Now as more and more of our genetic make-up is being discovered there is a possibility that people will seek to shift the blame on to their genes. 'I'm genetically wired towards stealing, so I could not help it.' 'My genes make me "oversexed" so I can't be to blame.' There is a world of difference, though, between a genetic inclination and being predetermined to an action. It seems certain that some of us are genetically wired for a tendency to a particular kind of behaviour, even some behaviours which corporately we regard as antisocial and criminal. However, we all remain free agents, able to choose whether or not we do behave that way. A genetic inclination to stealing does not force us to steal; we can make a choice, we cannot simply blame the genes.

Passing the buck is something we all do at times. For some people it appears to have become a complete way of life. The better way is to accept responsibility; to take the blame when it is deserved; to be honest about our failings. The truth is that we do not like admitting that we are sinners who fall short of God's glory. We do not want to admit that we have crossed the boundaries into wrongdoing. We prefer to think that we are okay really; we are not to blame. This shows up not only at a personal level but corporately. Global warming is caused largely through overconsumption of fossil fuels. But none of us likes to admit that we are to blame. We are keeping our homes at higher temperatures than we did even 20 years ago; we demand fresh fruit and vegetables from around the globe 365 days a year; we think nothing of driving for an hour or two just to go shopping. More and more air travel is contributing significantly to the greenhouse gas effect but we want our cheap flights, our weekend breaks to Europe and our holidays to all points around the globe. 'It's not me', we say, 'the plane would be going anyway so I might as well make sure it is full.' Our corporate failure to accept the blame for what we are doing to the planet is endangering the future for our children, grandchildren and for the planet as a whole.

Blame and vengeance

There is another side to blame completely. This is where someone else is to blame for something that has happened. The memories remain of the first time my family returned home to discover that our home had been burgled. Most of what had been taken was readily replaceable under our insurance policy. But there was a deep sense of violation that we all felt as we saw our clothes scattered across the floors where the drawers had been ransacked, and work files tipped out in the study. Then there was the deep sorrow at the jewellery which had been taken. It was not of great monetary value but the sentimental worth was great – and irreplaceable. We all felt angry. Some words were said about what we would like to do to the person(s) responsible if we were to find them. A desire for vengeance came rising to the surface.

There are a whole host of scenarios that we can draw here. A drunken car driver hits an innocent pedestrian and leaves her brain-damaged for life; he is to blame. A young man slips a drug into a young woman's drink and rapes her later, without her really recognizing what is happening; he is to blame. A teenage girl mugs a fellow teenager for a mobile phone; she is to blame. They can be far more harrowing than this. On my regular trips to Rwanda I have met those who saw their family killed before their eyes during the genocide of 1994. I have met those who are living with HIV/AIDS after being raped.

In any incidents like these there are guilty and innocent parties. The wronged person, the one sinned against, has a choice to make. The parents of the young pedestrian left with brain damage after a car accident have a choice to make. The victims of genocide or rape or mugging all have a choice to make. The blame is clear. But how to deal with it is the question left with the victims. A desire for revenge will almost certainly arise at some point; even if not immediately. Hatred for the perpetrator of the crime can grow inside the victim. The victim will make choices that allow the longing for vengeance or the hatred to develop; such feelings and thoughts can be buried away and rise to the surface again years later. They can be harboured, even cherished and nurtured, allowing the hatred to fester and to grow. Or they can make choices which are different. They can make choices for justice, and for forgiveness. They may even go on to making choices for reconciliation.

Confession and forgiveness

The blame game is one we all play. As we have seen, it takes two decidedly different forms. In one form it involves us seeking to shift the blame which is rightly ours away from ourselves and on to others, or on to the circumstances. Here we have a choice to make. We can choose to continually profess our innocence and keep shifting the blame. Or we can be honest, accept the blame, own up to it, face the possible consequences, and seek forgiveness. There is no other remedy to the temptation to pass the blame on to others. We can only overcome this temptation by admitting our wrongdoing, our guilt. This is called confession. Now the person whom above all we offend by passing the buck is God, so we need to confess to God. No complicated words are required; a simple cry for mercy is all that is needed (see the story of the Pharisee and the tax collector in Luke 18.9–14).

But there are times when it can be helpful to confess our sins to someone else so that they can declare God's forgiveness over us. This may be in some kind of formal setting with a minister/priest. But it equally may be less formal with a respected leader or friend. What is essential on such occasions is honesty in confession, and knowledge that the confessor will be wholly confidential and exhibit God's loving mercy.

There are certainly times when for real long-term healing it will be important to confess to the person whom we have wronged. This is hard to do. It is humbling and hurts. It also always runs the risk of the other person not offering us forgiveness; that is their decision and a risk that we have to take. This seeking reconciliation with others whom we have offended and hurt is part of what Jesus called us to do:

> So when you are offering your gift at the altar, if you remember that your brother or sister has something against you, leave your gift there before the altar and go; first be reconciled to your brother or sister, and then come and offer your gift.
>
> (Matthew 5.23–24)

It was the first day of the retreat at theological college. I had gone to the chapel to pray. I was clear that the retreat offered a real opportunity to seek God's guidance about the next phase of my ministry, which would also be the first as an ordained minister. I set myself to pray, to think and to read. For some reason I ended up praying in the vestry rather than the chapel. I was on my knees. As I prayed I kept finding my mind apparently wandering from my set task; instead of praying about my future it seemed my mind continually returned to an argument I had had recently with the Principal's wife. I kept trying to push this to one side. I can be very slow when it comes to recognizing the Holy Spirit's promptings – or was it stubbornness rather than slowness? Eventually I realized that God was trying to tell me that here was I offering my gift of my ministry on his altar while all the time there was a relationship that needed reconciliation first. I think I wrestled with God for quite some time about how it was her fault; how embarrassing it would be; how damaging it might be for me. But eventually I arose and went across, rather slowly and sheepishly, to the Principal's house. When no response came from the first ring of the bell I thought about leaving but knew I had to face this. I rang again. The Principal's wife came to the door. From her look I knew immediately that she understood why I was there. It was not an easy conversation but when I left I knew that reconciliation had taken place. I returned to the chapel vestry. Before long I found myself turning from intercession to thanksgiving and praise. I know that I have a vivid memory of this because the retreat did prove to be very decisive in helping me discern just where God was calling me next.

In blame's second form we are the innocent victims. The blame then rightly lies with another. We can choose in such circumstances to turn the blame into hatred, loathing or vengeance. Or we can choose to forgive. Forgiveness does not mean justice cannot or should not be done. Society has a responsibility to ensure, for example, that a murderer receives a due penalty for their crime. But the relatives of the victim can choose to forgive. They can choose to offer forgiveness, love, even friendship to the guilty person. This is exactly what has been happening in remarkable ways in some cases in Rwanda.

It was April 1994. During 100 days following the death of President Habyrimana around 800,000 people were killed. Among them a mother watched her two children slaughtered by a teenage boy. She will never forget his face. She will never have the image of the machete swinging down on her children time and again erased from her memory. She will never forget the inner longings to have died with them. She will never forget burying them.

Three years later, still grieving deeply, the widowed woman hears a knock. She opens the door of her mud brick house; she could never forget this face. The young man hangs his head in shame and begins to weep. His sorrow and grief pour out of him. Her anger boils up. She weeps, she shouts, she gesticulates wildly. She tells him how painful it has all been. She tells him where the children are buried. She asks him, 'Why?' He cannot explain. Eventually he turns to go. She asks him where he is living, what he is doing now that he has returned from the refugee camp. He tells her he is alone. His family were also killed. He has nothing. She invites him to stay; 'Be the son that you took away from me. Let me love you as my own son.' He stayed.

Jesus, blame and forgiveness

Jesus, as he hung on the cross, made a choice to forgive his killers and persecutors. 'Father, forgive them.' He made a choice to offer forgiveness to the dying thief. Forgiveness is never easy. It is always costly. The temptation to hang on to anger or bitterness or a sneaking thought of revenge goes with us continually.

Jesus had taught forgiveness throughout his ministry. He had taught of his Father as the great God of forgiveness. He had taught his disciples that just as they were forgiven so too they should forgive (Matthew 6.9–15). When Peter had tried to push

Jesus into giving limits to forgiveness Jesus had responded with a parable that made it quite clear that God's forgiveness is boundless (Matthew 18.21–35). He had spoken forgiveness into many lives. He had seen the transformation that forgiveness brings in the lives of adulterers, prostitutes, cheats, thieves and plain simple ordinary people (take a look, for example, at Mark 2.1–12; Luke 7.36–50 and John 8.1–11).

On the cross Jesus was pushed to the limit in terms of understanding and practising what he had taught and practised. On the cross, once again, he chose to forgive.

We, simply yet with so much difficulty, are called to do the same. When we find forgiveness tough we need to reflect afresh on the cross. This was what Jesus did to bring about our forgiveness. This is how much he forgives. We are the reason for his death. It is our blame, our wrongdoing, our sin which leads Jesus to give his life in sacrifice at the cross. In the Old Testament law there was an annual act involving the 'scapegoat'. The High Priest laid his hands on the goat and confessed the sins of the people over the goat; in this sense the sins are 'laid on the goat'. The goat is then sent into the desert and the sins of the people are taken away with him; they therefore 'escape' what their sins deserve. On the cross Jesus acts as 'scapegoat' for our sins. We are the ones to blame; yet he takes the blame. We are the ones who deserve death; yet he dies. In his death he brings about our forgiveness. Having been forgiven he calls on us to forgive those who have sinned against us. In light of what he did at the cross how can we do any less than forgive?

Ideas for reflection

1 Consider examples of how and when you seek to shift the blame.
2 Are there instances where you are harbouring hurt, hatred, a desire for vengeance that need to be brought to the foot of the cross?
3 Do you need to take any action to offer/express forgiveness to someone? How best might this be done?

Pictures

Jesus Mafa: *Pharisee and Publican* and *Unforgiving Servant*
Dinah Roe Kendall: *The Unmerciful Servant*
Sidney Spencer: *The Hens*

Prayer

I blame my parents, my friends, the church, the government, the
environment. I blame you, Lord! It's not my fault!

Help me, Lord, to take the blame when I should. Give me the courage
to own up, to confess, to say sorry, to change.

And when others are to blame help me with my hurt; enable me
to forgive, just as you have forgiven me. Amen.

14

Going at God's pace

I love the title of the book, *The Three Mile an Hour God*. It reflects the simple fact that when God became human in Jesus of Nazareth his ministry and life were conducted at walking pace. No cars, trains, planes or even horses. Jesus walked everywhere (that is part of why his ride on a donkey into Jerusalem, on what we call Palm Sunday, was so significant; it was a deliberate change and fulfilled the words of the prophets). This is not to say that Jesus' life was never busy. The Gospels make it quite clear that he had to deal with crowds, huge crowds, on a regular basis. There were times when he and the disciples were so pressed that they did not have time to eat. Busy-ness and pressure have not just arrived with the modern pace of life; they have always existed in one form or another. I am intrigued by how Jesus handled this, travelling at just three miles per hour.

I have long been fascinated too by the clear sense of purpose, direction and timing that the Gospels display Jesus as having. John's Gospel is particularly clear with its frequent references to 'My hour has not yet come' (John 2.4; 7.6, 8, 30; 8.20) and then the climactic, 'The hour has come' in 12.23, and the even more climactic, 'it is finished' of 19.30. Before considering these thoughts in more detail let us consider our temptations that connect with this. These are the temptations to go too fast, or too slow; the temptations to run ahead of God, or to drag behind.

As a family we have enjoyed many walks over the years. When the children were very tiny Rosemary and I would carry them on our backs up hills and along cliff edges. We have memories of some fairly hairy moments with small children close to steep edges. My tendency, with my long legs, has always been to stride out and forget that others' legs are rather shorter than my own. It is now edging towards pay-back time so far as this is concerned. I do not walk much slower but I am not as fit as I once was, or should be now. The adult children all walk more quickly. Now it is not unusual for Rosemary and me to be left at the back while the young adults stride out. They do not all share an equal love of walking but when they do it they don't go at a snail's pace! In our walk with God we can sometimes be drawn into walking, or even running, ahead of the pace at which God wants us to go; or we can be tempted to drag behind and suggest that he is trying to take us too far, too fast. This is true for us personally, but is also often true of how we feel and think as church congregations. What we all have to learn is how to keep in step with the Spirit.

Two well-known church leaders were standing on a city street. One was waving his arms around very enthusiastically; there was a wide grin on his face and the words were flowing. The other stood, attentively, listening. He hardly managed to get a single word in for the 10 minutes that passed. One who had seen the incident asked the quiet partner about it later. The answer was:

'Well, that's him, a hundred great ideas before breakfast which he has to share. The trouble is that ninety-eight or ninety-nine of them are absolutely hopeless. But there are always one or two which are potential gems, filled with divine inspiration. It's my job to discern the one or two because he really struggles to tell the difference himself. But I'd never think of them myself in a month of Sundays.'

They made a great partnership. Some of those one or two have proved over the years to be hugely significant internationally, let alone in their own local setting. The temptation for the entrepreneur-enthusiast was to race ahead and, frankly, then cause mayhem. The temptation for the other was to see all the difficulties, dangers and problems so that they never moved ahead at all or missed the right moment to do so.

For most of us, for most of our lives, serving God faithfully is about walking with Jesus day by day at a regular sustainable pace. Most are called to fulfil our vocation in life by being the best spouse, parent and child that we can be. For most of us our calling from God is to serve him well by serving others in our work; whether that be as a secretary, street cleaner, bank manager, shop assistant, teacher, musician or whatever. Where he places us and calls us to be we are to be living witnesses of the love of God for those with whom we work; do our work for his glory; and seek his kind of justice. Outside of paid work we are called to be engaged in our local community and share in the life of a local fellowship in worship and prayer. We are not to divide our lives up into separate compartments labelled 'family', 'work', 'church' and 'leisure'. We are called to be serving God in everything that we do. This means then that development and progression in life is normally one step at a time. We cannot learn to run before we can walk. We learn how to be a child as we go through life. The role changes as we move from our earliest years into adolescence and then into adulthood. It changes again as our parents age and become frail and more dependent. Honouring our parents is a lifelong calling, but we learn what is involved each step of the way, and it changes over the years. The same, naturally, applies to learning to be a parent; and how to be a husband or wife. None of these callings in life are ever static; we keep changing and developing as individuals, so how we relate to one another also changes. Yet through all the changes the parent is called to care for and support the child. The husband and wife are called to live in faithful commitment to each other. These roles will not always be glamorous or exciting. There will be times when they seem mundane, boring even and then temptations to 'get out' can come. But the call of God is faithfully to walk with him.

Pete arrived on the team with a bang. He was lively, bright, chatty and full of ideas. It was wonderful to welcome him. His energy and enthusiasm were all that a leadership could hope for in a new, young team member. He related well to other team members, and the children loved him. Then things started to go slightly wrong. It was not hugely noticeable at first; it was put down to inexperience, and the energy covered over the cracks. But as the week rolled on it became clear that actually more and more of the team were struggling with Pete. Some of the children were also not racing to be with him the way that they had been initially. Pete's problem was that he was trying to run before he could walk. He had never done anything quite like this before; but he was sure that he knew how to handle things. He struggled with advice, however, gently offered. He seemed to have an unwillingness to learn. He thought he could lead without learning from others, without experience and without reflecting on what was happening around him. Pete had all the gifts and attributes necessary to develop into a very fine leader of children's work. But he was determined, it seemed, to race ahead of how God wanted to develop and grow him. Oak trees last hundreds of years, but they grow slowly. Christian leaders, by and large, grow into their leadership through learning from others, through experience and through step-by-step development. The temptation can be to try and race ahead of God's development plan.

Mary, on the other hand, on the same team and at the same time, initially seemed rather quiet, a little shy. She did not immediately leap to the front, or stand out in conversation. However, as the week passed it became clear that she was remarkably good at getting alongside both children and fellow team members. She would quietly notice a job that needed doing and offer to get it done. In reviewing the whole week she showed remarkable insight, and had some great ideas for the future. Next time around she was given more responsibility, though she was not sure about taking it on. Her confidence grew, her skills developed and the leadership potential became ever clearer. A few years on she now takes a leading role. She still has much to learn; there remains in her a tendency to hold back when she needs to step forward. That is the temptation that faces her; to go more slowly than God might want her to go.

Two very different characters placed in the same setting; both with huge potential for growth and leadership. One tries to run before he can walk; the other in danger of dragging behind. One needs to learn the importance of taking time to learn and develop; the other in danger of underestimating her God-given potential. I believe that our genetic make-up and our life experiences will tend to mean that we are each more likely to be tempted either to race ahead or to drag behind. However, both temptations can come to all of us at different times.

Step by step or leaping the chasm

The very nature of how this chapter has progressed so far is descriptive of my own make-up. It has emphasized the step-by-step nature of growth and development. It has noted the call to daily faithfulness. This reflects my own personal tendency to take things carefully. I am a reflector; I like to investigate and research properly. I want to carry everyone with me in a group, or as a church. In this sense I tend to seek to exercise power primarily through affiliation. Team work is important to me. When standing at the top of the Tarzan jump at Go Ape I am one of those who think about it, see the possible dangers and am unsure I want the experience. I edge my way into the cold sea. I am not naturally an adventurer or a risk-taker. Yet surprisingly as I look back my life has been filled with adventure, risk and excitement. Rosemary and I met and married in 10 months. I found myself in Russia taking pioneering steps with Scripture Union there. I helped instigate the Children's Workers Training Conferences in Siberia. I travel to Rwanda, Uganda and Burundi regularly – and love to do so. There have been a host of fresh initiatives with which I have been engaged. For while not a natural risk-taker I am someone who it seems God has called to be a visionary. Detail can bore me but vision and the big picture thrill my heart.

One of the most remarkable Christian organizations to have developed over the past 10 years, I think, is Viva Network. The passion for, and commitment to, working with children at risk all over the globe has been outstanding. It is largely due, under God, to the vision, passion and entrepreneurship of one man, Patrick McDonald. I am indebted to him for this next phrase which he included in a note to me, 'You don't, after all, leap a chasm in small steps . . . you jump!' Sometimes the size of the task that faces us, the challenge that lies before us, is so great that we have to make giant leaps of faith. There can be points in life where God calls us to make a major change, and there is only one way to make it; that's to take the leap.

This happens to church communities as well. A fellowship can be going along quite happily in ways that it has done for years, with gentle adjustments along the way. Then it becomes clear that in order to serve the community in which it is set it needs to do things quite differently. Incremental change will not be enough; there has to be a radical change. This requires a leap of faith. The same could be true for an entire denomination, including my own. When faced with major change the temptation to stay put and play safe will always be strong. We like our comfort zones. We feel safe and secure in them. We become anxious about what the future might look like with radical change; fear of the unknown and unexpected creeps or floods in; so we choose to stay with what we know. But sometimes God's call turns our whole world upside down and as we say 'Yes' to this call we discover God's love and power in whole new ways which we would miss if we stayed put.

Jesus at his Father's pace

When he was in the Temple at the age of 12 Jesus was very clear with his parents: 'Did you not know that I must be in my Father's house?' (Luke 2.49). But he returned to Nazareth recognizing that his place was still there living under his parents' authority. Over the years that followed as he heard the Scriptures read, pondered on them and prayed, his understanding of what the Father wanted him to do developed. This development must have taken shape also through conversation with his parents, and with members of his local community and synagogue. His regular visits to Jerusalem for the festivals; his work and observation of life around him all also impacted his understanding.

There then comes the point where he discerns it is time to leave. The first 30 years were step by step, but now there is a chasm to leap. He has reached the chasm step by step but leaving home and being baptized by John is a leap that takes him to a whole new place from which there can be no return.

His ministry begins to unfold; at Cana Mary asks him to help at the wedding; he is reluctant to do so: 'My hour has not yet come' (John 2.4). But Mary knows that the new phase has begun and she encourages him on. He grows in popularity through his teaching and miracles; the crowd want him to take a leap into kingship, but he knows this is not the way and he must still travel step by step (John 6.1–15). His brothers, not convinced about him, want him to make a display of power and popularity; yet Jesus knows that this will precipitate greater opposition and the time for this has not yet arrived, so he goes to Jerusalem quietly rather than with a fanfare (John 7.1–10). He keeps teaching, preaching and healing. He continually nurtures his disciples. When they come to recognize him as the Messiah, then he begins to teach them about the necessity for him to suffer and to die; and he tells them that he will be raised from death. Finally three years into this public journey he makes another leap; instead of walking he rides into Jerusalem on a donkey, and the crowds hail him as the Messiah, as the deliverer King (John 12.12–16). In the midst of all the noise and acclamation some Gentiles seek Jesus out (John 12.20–28). This acts as a sign for him that the hour has arrived; he came to be the Saviour of the world (John 3.14–20) and the world is now being drawn to him. So he continues through his final week to act and speak in ways which he knows will lead to his arrest, trial and crucifixion. He steps boldly forward and then leaps the chasm to his death. He resists all temptations to choose another way, to play it safe, to avoid the pain. He travels at his Father's pace throughout. Then in his Father's time he is raised to life. In his Father's time he appears to the disciples in a variety of ways and in a variety of places. In his Father's time he is taken up into heaven. In his Father's time the Holy Spirit is sent upon the assembled disciples, the Church, so that they and it too can travel at the Father's pace.

Travelling on

Some of us are cautious by nature; others are adventurous, impetuous. We need each other and have to learn from one another. The cautious ones need to be encouraged sometimes to take a leap of faith; the adventurous and impetuous ones sometimes need to be helped to slow down, take others with them and ensure the journey is properly prepared. All of us, personally and together, will continually be tempted to run ahead or to drag behind, to play safe and stay secure rather than step out into God's continual adventure. What we all need to do is to learn to travel at God's pace knowing that for much of life and most of the time he calls us to live faithfully where we are step by step, but that there come occasions where he also calls us to take leaps of faith across the chasms.

Ideas for reflection

1 By temperament are you more prone to running ahead or dragging behind? What factors have made you this way?
2 Where do you see the temptations to play safe in your own/ your church's life?
3 What might help you keep in step with the Spirit?
4 What might help you make a leap of faith when that is what is called for?

Pictures

Jesus Mafa: *Jesus at Twelve*; *Wedding at Cana*
Dinah Roe Kendall: *Jesus visits Bethany*

Sidney Spencer: *Rising from Sleep in the Morning* or *Driven by the Spirit*

Prayer

Thank you for the quiet, silent years of Jesus' life. Thank you for the steadiness and simplicity of your preparation of him for his public ministry and his sacrifice on the cross. Thank you that he walked in step with the Spirit day by day. Help me to do the same. Help me to walk at your pace through life. Help me to take the leaps of faith when you call me to do so. Help me to keep in step with the Spirit. Amen.

15

Giving up and endurance

In 2005 the BBC broadcast a noteworthy documentary series charting the journey of a group of adults with a variety of physical disabilities. The group contained adults who were blind, deaf, artificially limbed and wheelchair-bound. Together they crossed part of Central America. They started on the Atlantic coast and finished at the Pacific. En route they went through jungle; they climbed up and down mountains, crossed fast-flowing rivers and endured all kinds of pain, trauma and anguish. It was an extraordinary journey, and a stunning feat. It was an example of enormous courage, endurance and teamwork. While it was gruelling physically, it was a more remarkable achievement in terms of the emotional challenge that it presented to all concerned. As human beings, we are capable of quite amazing powers of endurance when we choose to put our minds and wills to the task.

It was 1989 and Billy Graham's Mission to London was fast approaching. At the time I was working with Scripture Union as Inner London Evangelist. My main brief was to help churches of all kinds across inner London to develop their work with children, young people and families. There was a particular concern to develop work with those who were not regularly part of any church life. Since my brief was London, when SU were approached to help with the children's side of the Billy Graham Mission I was asked to take on the role. It was hard work, but also a great deal of fun. Our small working group had memories of the Luis Palau Mission to London a few years earlier. During this there had been a large children's event at Queens Park Rangers'

Loftus Road ground. This had been organized by some of my SU colleagues. As a group we thought it would be good to do something similar for BG. But there were difficulties to overcome. The Billy Graham Evangelistic Association (BGEA) had never run a children's event as part of one of Billy's missions before. So they were unsure about it. They were even less sure about where it would fit into the schedule.

Eventually, after much debate, it was agreed that such an event should be staged. In fact it was agreed that there should be two events, the first at West Ham's ground, Upton Park, and the second in the Earls Court Arena. It was quite a project to plan. Writers, presenters and performers to find, scenery to be produced and an event in which thousands of children, along with their parents, could actively participate, enjoy and hear something of the good news of Jesus Christ. Early on it became clear that Billy himself would not be able to make an appearance. The traumas we had working with the Metropolitan Police, London Transport, local managers, fire officers, let alone the BGEA, were endless. Several times we really thought that we would have to call the whole thing off. But every time we reached that point somehow we found the energy and inspiration to solve a problem and keep going. The pressure was seriously added to by Rosemary expecting and giving birth to our third child, Andrew, during the whole period. This meant three under-fives at home.

The outdoor event at West Ham came first. The sun shone, the crowds came, the fire officer gave us the go-ahead 30 minutes before the start and it worked. Bubble Trouble blew into life and action. I have vivid memories a few days later of trying to sleep on the floor of a Portakabin inside Earls Court Arena with my stage manager and SU colleague, Michael Wells. Just before BG, Earls Court had staged the Royal Tournament and immediately following there was to be a huge opera production. Around 4.30 a.m. Mike and I arose to begin setting up. We just sat there and looked at each other, 'What on earth are we doing? Here we are, two amateurs, producing an event for thousands of children in the Earls

Court Arena with no such previous experience. We must be mad.' No chance to give up at that point; the show had to go on. It worked again – and we had the whole lot cleared away in time for the final rally that Saturday evening. The whole experience taught me huge amounts about endurance, sticking at a task and seeing it through, even though on many occasions the best thing to do, certainly the easiest, seemed to be to give up.

I hope that this particular story brought at least a flicker of a smile to your face. It was very hard work; it did take a great deal of patient endurance. Yet it was a great deal of fun. There were a lot of laughs on the way; and the joy and excitement of the events themselves live on in my memory. Keeping going and not giving up are not always about the grimmer side of life. They have to take place in everyday life. Getting to work on time and doing the job; caring for the children; running a home; ensuring that the local church is ready for worship week in and week out are all examples of where we all have to keep going. Every one of us has our moments when we feel like giving up, running away or escaping but the call is to be faithful, steadfast and to patiently endure. Where God has given us a task to do he calls us to do it to the best of our ability, in his Spirit's strength and to keep at it until he calls us to stop and do something else.

For some, however, the call to endure can be very wearing, painful and costly. Caring year after year for a severely disabled child requires enormous patience and love. I have been humbled and amazed at how friends have done this with their children. The same applies to caring for the elderly, especially when they develop a disease such as Alzheimer's. Living with the tragedy and sadness of seeing someone previously able and active now not knowing what is happening around them is a costly care. The same applies to those who care for sufferers of diseases like motor-neurone. How often there must be the temptation to give up; to pack it all in, or even to try and end it all. Patiently loving and caring through the tiredness, the grief and the pain come as God's call.

There have been Christians throughout the centuries who have also been called upon to patiently endure suffering for the sake of Jesus Christ. This was the situation for the Christians to whom the book of Revelation was written. There is a refrain through the book: 'Here is a call for the endurance and faith of the saints' (Revelation 13.10; 14.12). Such suffering for the faith of Jesus Christ still continues. One who converts to Christ from Islam or Orthodox Judaism faces being cut off from the family. In some nations Christians are still deliberately kept out of jobs, placed in poor housing or refused access to education. Some Christian leaders still face imprisonment, and torture for their faith. Under such duress the temptation to give up, to disown Jesus and to opt for the easy road will look very inviting. Yet the call of Christ is to stay faithful and to keep going.

Jesus' test of avoiding suffering and the cross

All of which leads us to reflect that the key temptation throughout Jesus' ministry was the temptation to avoid suffering and the cross. It is spelled out quite specifically for us at the time of Peter's confession at Caesarea Philippi in Luke 9.18–27, Matthew 16.13–23 and Mark 8.27–38. Peter recognizes Jesus as the Messiah. Immediately Jesus begins to teach and explain how he must suffer and die. Peter steps in to say that this cannot be. Jesus' reaction is very strong: 'Get behind me, Satan!' He recognizes in Peter's words the attempt of the devil to deflect him once again from the course his Father has set. He is being tempted to go another way than the way of the cross.

It is a temptation Jesus knew would face his disciples continually. Would they, and we, take the easy way or the way of the cross (Mark 13.12f.; John 11.7–10)? Will we give in to the temptation to either give up all together – Luke 8.13 – or choose the easy life – Luke 8.14? Will we prefer self-defence and protection rather than the costliness of taking up our cross and following him?

This then leads us towards Jesus in the Garden of Gethsemane and at the cross. For there we see him tested to the limit and coming through.

For a long while Jesus had been speaking to his disciples of how 'he must go to Jerusalem and undergo great suffering at the hands of the elders and chief priests and scribes, and be killed, and on the third day be raised' (Matthew 16.21). Luke describes Jesus as so determined that 'he set his face to go to Jerusalem' (Luke 9.51, recalling Isaiah 50.7: 'I have set my face like flint . . .').

Now he knows that the time of trial and death is upon him. Judas Iscariot, one of the Twelve, has gone to betray him. He knows the end has arrived.

In Gethsemane Jesus takes Peter, James and John to be close to him as he prays. He describes himself as 'deeply grieved, even to death', or as the NIV puts it, 'overwhelmed with sorrow to the point of death' (Matthew 26.38). What inner anguish there was as he contemplated the crucifixion which he knew awaited him.

Then he prays. He prostrates himself face down in prayer. The prayer, at this late, late stage has few words and is very clear: 'My Father (Abba), if it is possible, let this cup pass from me; yet not what I want but what you want' (Matthew 26.39). The intimacy of prayer with his Father is as strong as ever. The request straightforward – if there is another way; if there is a way of my not drinking this cup from your hand – then let me go that way.

This is a real longing to find a way out of the pain and anguish of the trial and the cross. But the determination remains firm: 'Yet not what I want but what you want.'

Long before this, after speaking with the Samaritan woman at the well, Jesus had said to his disciples, 'My food is to do the will of him who sent me and to complete his work' (John 4.34). That passion and commitment does not diminish even in the midst of the deepest and fiercest longing to go a different way if at all possible.

The reference to 'cup' is important. Earlier, Matthew tells us (Matthew 20.22–23), Jesus had talked with the disciples of the cup he had to drink. This would seem to be a reference to Isaiah 51.17, 22 and Jeremiah 49.12 which speak of the cup of God's wrath; though Psalm 16.5 uses the cup as an image of God's salvation. Given the nature of what Jesus is about to undergo the image of taking into himself the wrath of God against sin seems clear. But then this very act will prove to be the cup of salvation for us all. Jesus perceived himself to be entering into the suffering which was God's wrath against human sin: 'the Son of Man did not come to be served but to serve, and to give his life a ransom for many' (Mark 10.45).

The fact that he prays this again and again emphasizes simply how overwhelming was the anguish. Luke tells us that Jesus 'in his anguish . . . prayed more earnestly, and his sweat became like great drops of blood falling down on the ground' (Luke 22.44).

When the going is at its very toughest the temptation to give up, or find a way out that is easier, is always going to be very strong. We will never manage to handle such a test unless we have been through many tough ones before. The way to handle them is to know that what we are doing is in line with the Father's will, which Jesus discerned from the Scriptures. And we will also have to learn from Jesus that prayer will always be at the heart of how we can handle the very toughest of tests.

In prayer we are seeking to align our wills with God's will so that the choice of 'My way or God's way' in a sense disappears, for we will want God's way to be our way. In one sense, because our will has been aligned exactly with the Father's, 'My way will be God's way.' By the Spirit the Father will have shaped my will into exact alliance with his. But this kind of enduring, anguished prayer does not just develop overnight. For Jesus this is the culmination of a life of prayer. The one who we see through the Gospels drawing aside from the busy-ness of his ministry to be alone with his Father has been learning in prayer all the way along. So too we need to be those who are continually learning in prayer, by praying – there is no other way to learn how to pray. Then when the deepest and toughest tests come there will be a wellspring of prayer on which we can draw. For we will never hold fast to the way of the cross without being in prayer with the Father.

The test of endurance is one to which we are all called. No follower of Jesus is exempt from this calling. Again let us listen to the writer to the Hebrews:

> Therefore, since we are surrounded by so great a cloud of witnesses, let us also lay aside every weight and the sin that clings so closely, and let us run with perseverance the race that is set before us, looking to Jesus the pioneer and perfecter of our faith, who for the sake of the joy that was set before him endured the cross, disregarding its shame, and has taken his seat at the right hand of the throne of God. Consider him who endured such hostility against himself from sinners, so that you may not grow weary or lose heart.
>
> (Hebrews 12.1–3)

Finally we turn to the simple truth that Jesus stayed on the cross. He was tempted to prove himself by coming down from it. His opponents taunt him with the very idea:

> You who would destroy the temple and build it in three days, save yourself! If you are the Son of God, come down from the cross ... He saved others; he cannot save himself. He is the King of Israel; let him come down from the cross now, and we will believe in him.
>
> (Matthew 27.40–41)

The scribes and elders are still appealing for a sign from him! He could have done as they said. But he knew that to do so would be to fail to carry the sins of the world. He knew that to destroy the evil one and death, to be the victorious one, he had to die. He knew that the Lamb had to be sacrificed; the scapegoat had to go. The temple of his body had to be destroyed so that in three days it could be raised again. He knew that the way of redemption was through his death; there was no other way. So he endured the cross – for you and for me.

Finishing the race

Jesus endured to the end. He trusted that the Father would triumph through his suffering; he relied on his Father to vindicate him rather than try and vindicate himself. He held on to his conviction that death would be defeated by his going through death; that the evil one would be overcome by his own submission to the ultimate consequences of evil, the abandonment of God. His vindication came with the resurrection; his triumph over death was revealed in his new life.

The call of God's Church, the call of each follower of Jesus is to endure to the end, to finish the race. The Christian life is certainly much more like a marathon than a sprint; it is more like a triathlon than a marathon. It does not require simply quick bursts of energy but year-by-year, month-by-month, day-by-day, moment-by-moment faithfulness to Jesus Christ. The temptation to give up will come frequently and look very attractive. Contemplating and relying on the cross will be our strength, knowing that his resurrection guarantees ours.

Ideas for reflection

1 Recall one or two occasions when you have been tempted to give up. What kept you going?
2 Think of examples of Christians you know who shine out as examples of patient endurers. What might you learn from their lives?
3 Reread one of the accounts of Jesus in Gethsemane, on trial, and of his crucifixion. Contemplate how he endured.

Pictures

Jesus Mafa: *Gethsemane* and *The Crucifixion*
Dinah Roe Kendall: *Garden of Gethsemane*
Sidney Spencer: *He Departed into a Mountain to Pray*

Prayer

Almighty God,
whose most dear one went not up to joy but first he suffered pain,
and entered not into glory before he was crucified:
mercifully grant that we, walking in the way of the cross,
may find it none other than the way of life and peace;
through Jesus Christ your Son our Lord,
who is alive and reigns with you,
in the unity of the Holy Spirit,
one God, now and for ever. Amen.
          (Collect for the Third Sunday of Lent, *Common Worship*)

Lord God,
whose blessed Son our Saviour
gave his back to the smiters
and did not hide his face from shame:
give us grace to endure the sufferings of this present time
with sure confidence in the glory that shall be revealed;
through Jesus Christ our Lord. Amen.
                    (Post Communion Prayer, Fourth Sunday of Lent,
                                        Common Worship)

16

Lead us not into temptation

-------♦-------

Temptation takes thousands of different forms when it comes to specific examples. Yet it has a great commonality to it which crosses all times and cultures. Temptation is not wrong; it is part of what it means to be human. Every temptation comes, in one way or another, as a test, an opportunity for growth and discovery about ourselves, our world, other people and above all about God.

As we draw to a conclusion the question that is left is this: 'Are there principles that help us not simply resist the temptations that come our way but also to grow and mature through them as tests?' In reflecting on Jesus there are some such principles that have arisen time and again.

Knowing our identity in God

When Jesus was driven out by the Spirit into the wilderness to be tempted by Satan the primary temptation was to doubt his identity as the Son of God. In two of the temptations Satan begins, 'If you are the Son of God' (Matthew 4.3, 6). The temptation placed before Jesus is to question and doubt the declaration made by God at Jesus' baptism, 'You are my Son, the Beloved' (Luke 3.22). Throughout his life Jesus had been learning and discovering his identity. Like every child he would have asked his parents, 'Where did I come from?' 'How was I born?' Like every parent, Mary and Joseph would have had to make a judgement about how much they told their son and explained to him about the origins of his life.

Somewhere along the line they must have told him the story of Gabriel appearing to Mary; of the appearance to Joseph in a dream, and of all the events around his birth in Bethlehem. He had to grasp his true identity as son of Mary and Joseph; but also as son of God. The incident Luke gives us of Jesus at the age of 12 in Jerusalem shows us his developing understanding. He knows that he has a special relationship with God as his Father. He knows he has a special calling. But it is not fully understood. The baptism acts as a decisive point of confirmation of his identity. This identity is tested throughout his public ministry but it is his sense of being secure in it which is key to Jesus being able to continue to resist temptation and live as he does.

For every disciple of Jesus being secure in our identity lies at the heart of how we stand firm and are able to resist temptation. Our identity comes both from how God has made us, and what he has done for us in Christ. God 'makes' us unique through the genetic processes that occur in our being formed in the womb. Each of us is an extraordinary mixture of our parents' genes, which are themselves inherited from their parents. So how we look, our size and our natural abilities all come from God as a gift in creation. It is not just this genetic make-up which is God-given. So too are the circumstances into which we are born. All of us are shaped by our homes, our ethnicity, nationality, the community in which we grow up and so much more besides. At one level it is an 'accident of birth' that I am living in the wealthy part of the world. At another level God has placed me in this setting.

To be secure in this part of my identity I have to learn, as I grow and develop, what my gifts, abilities and weaknesses are. I will be shaped by life's circumstances and events and I need to continually try and understand who I am. This is a lifelong journey. The very writing of this book has raised long-forgotten memories that I recognize have shaped me into being the person that I am today. The clearer the self-knowledge and understanding, the more secure I can be as a person.

But alongside this I know there are parts of me that are decidedly unpleasant and ungodly. I have said, thought and done things throughout my life which can be described only as 'sin'. I have also been scarred and marred by the sins of others. So I need forgiveness and cleansing. I need renewal and regeneration. This is where security in Christ is key. In Christ God has declared me not guilty; he has put me into a right relationship with himself (Romans 3.21–26; 5.6–11). In Christ I have been adopted into God's family; I am his beloved child (Romans 8.15–17; Galatians 3.26—4.7). In Christ I have been sealed by the Holy Spirit and set apart for God for ever (Ephesians 1.3–14). In Christ I have been declared to be a saint and part of God's royal priesthood and holy nation (1 Peter 1.3–9; 2.4–10). In Christ God has declared that I have eternal life (John 3.16; 1 John 5.11–12). It is an amazing thing to be loved by God and to know that I am his for ever. This is the ultimate security for us all; not our own efforts or abilities but God's amazing grace lavished upon us in Jesus Christ. When Jesus died on the cross I died with him and all my sin and rebellion was dealt with once and for all. When Jesus was raised from death I was raised with him so my future resurrection is secure. Given all of this then nothing, not even the greatest powers of darkness, can separate me from God's love (Romans 8.31–39).

Being clear and firm in our identity in Christ is the rock on which we stand in resisting temptation.

Knowing our calling under God

Our identity in Christ is specific but it is also general. Every believer is equally a child of God. All disciples are given new life by the Holy Spirit. All in Christ are saints and belong to his royal priesthood. But alongside of this comes God's specific calling on each one of us. This is rooted in the person that he has created through our genetic make-up, and the way we have developed through life's circumstances. Yet as we enter into living faith and grow in it we also discover that God gives fresh gifts to us. He gives us our natural talents, and expects us to use them for his glory through serving the world and our neighbour. He also gives specific gifts of the Holy Spirit to help us further in serving him. These gifts are written about by Paul in 1 Corinthians 7.12–14; Romans 12; 1 Thessalonians 5.19–20 and Ephesians 4. Peter writes about them in 1 Peter 4.7–11. Some of these gifts once given to a person may remain with them for life. But I have certainly known the experience for myself, and I have seen it in others, where a gift is given at a specific time for a specific need. These are after all gifts of God distributed by the Spirit as he chooses.

However, through this complex mixture of our natural talents, life's experiences and opportunities and the gifts of the Spirit, God gives each of us specific callings on our lives. These are discovered through practice; the observations of others; inner conviction and calling; and the recognition of God's people. I am sure that knowing our God-given calling in life is a further essential key in helping us resist temptation. Jesus was very clear, 'the Son can do nothing on his own, but only what he sees the Father doing' (John 5.19). He knew his calling and he remained firmly focussed on fulfilling it. As we become clear in what God calls us to do so we will be better equipped to resist the temptation to become either lazy or overactive. We will focus on fulfilling the Father's will for our lives.

Scripture

When the risen Lord Jesus appears to his disciples, Luke makes it very clear that his explanation of his suffering and death were to be understood through the Scriptures (Luke 24.25–27, 32, 44–49). At the outset of his public ministry Jesus' manifesto was drawn from the Scriptures (Luke 4.16–21). When tempted by Satan in the wilderness each time Jesus' response came from the Scriptures (Luke 4.1–12). Jesus' understanding of his own identity as the Messiah who was to be the Suffering Servant came from his reading of, and reflection on, the Scriptures. His understanding of his call to go to the cross came from his reflection on the Scriptures.

Since he is our example then the Scriptures must play a prominent part in our ability to handle temptation. It is from our reading and study of Scripture that we discover our identity in Christ; it is here too that we will discern our calling under God. It is through the Scriptures that we learn how to discern right from wrong. It is in them that we discover God's wisdom for living and staying faithful even in the darkest and toughest times.

So personal Bible reading and study must always play a key part in Christian living. There are no definitive set ways of doing this. A whole host of methods exist and have proved to be of value to people down through the centuries and across cultures. The essential point is to make time to allow the written word of God to shape our thinking and our lives so that we are able to live godly lives. But no individual can grasp the depths and wonders of the Bible on their own. So studying the Bible with another person or within a group adds to our learning and understanding. Listening to the Bible being read in worship, and hearing someone explain it through a sermon, are also major ways of allowing God to speak to us through the pages of Scripture.

It is as we immerse ourselves in the Scriptures that we become able to know what speaks to each situation we face. Jesus was able in the desert to recall relevant texts from Deuteronomy because of his lifelong listening to the Scriptures at the synagogue, and engaging in discussion with others about them there (as we see illustrated when he is just 12 in the Temple – Luke 2.41–50). He did not have the freedom to carry a small Bible around in his pocket; we do. The Scriptures need to be constantly in our lives if we are to really grow through the temptations and tests that come our way.

Prayer

Jesus' contemplation of his call often took place in prayer. He regularly prayed alone. He prayed with others formally in the synagogue. He prayed with his disciples, and invited them to pray with him. Since we see him praying all night just before he chooses the Twelve it would appear clear that part of his praying was seeking his Father's guidance and wisdom for decisions that had to be made (Luke 6.12–14). His prayer in Gethsemane is a mixture of pleading for a different way, for being in line with the Father's will, and for strength to fulfil it (Luke 22.39–45). Prayer was at the heart of Jesus' spiritual life. It therefore needs to be at the heart of ours.

Jesus gave his disciples a pattern of prayer. We know it as the Lord's Prayer. Within this prayer we find him teaching us to pray, 'Lead us not into temptation, But deliver us from evil' (Matthew 6.13; Luke 11.4, RSV). As he enters Gethsemane he tells Peter, James and John to 'pray that you may not enter temptation' (Luke 22.40, RSV). Now given everything we have looked at in this book, what exactly did Jesus mean? Given that temptation is part of our human experience and the Gospels themselves are clear that Jesus himself was led into the wilderness to be tempted, what are we praying when we say, 'Lead us not into temptation'? James is very clear in his letter that God does not 'tempt' anyone (James 1.13). God does, however, very clearly test us, and he leads us into places and times of testing. He does so to teach us and strengthen us.

When we pray these words of the Lord's Prayer we are asking God not to lead or take us into a place of testing which is beyond what we can bear in his strength and power. We are asking him to protect us from temptation from within ourselves, from the world around us and from the evil one which would be beyond our capacity to withstand. So we are praying that God will always provide us with 'a way of escape' (see 1 Corinthians 10.13). But we are praying more than this. We are praying also that God will help us to grow through the tests that temptation sets us. Then finally the whole prayer is set with the final end in view. It looks to the day when God's kingdom will come in all its fullness; it looks to the day of judgement. In this petition we are praying that God will also keep us and deliver us on that great and final day of judgement. It is a wonderful prayer. We can never pray it too often for

our whole lives will be filled with temptation and we need God's
protection, strength and deliverance every step of the way.

Mutual support and encouragement

Our prayer, 'Lead us not into temptation', also spurs us on to remember that the experience of temptation is one we share together.
Since 'no testing has overtaken you that is not common to everyone' (1 Corinthians 10.13), then we should be able to help one
another in resisting and handling the temptations that come
our way. We do not struggle alone, but together. In the midst of
a particular temptation we might feel alone but in learning how
to resist and respond to temptation we can, and must, help one
another through mutual support and encouragement. This can
happen only where we are willing to be honest, open and transparent with one another. This is difficult for most of us to do.
We all like to put on a good image of ourselves. We do not like
revealing the darker side of our characters and thoughts. The fact
that all of us face temptations seems lost on us when it comes to
this point. Somehow we continually convince ourselves that our
thoughts of violence, greed, sexual fantasy, doubt and fear must
be far worse than those of anyone else we know. We fear what
people will think of us if we reveal our true inner selves.

Now I am not advocating here a great public revelation all the
time of our deepest temptations; that would not be helpful.
However, all of us do need someone, or a small group of people,
with whom we can be totally honest and vulnerable. Such people
need to be those whom we can trust to hold confidences; they must
be people who we know will accept us as we are, not condemn us,
and will help us know forgiveness and fresh strength from God.
For some people a formal relationship with a confessor will be an
essential aspect of this. Others will find this in less formal ways
with a soul friend, or a small prayer group. This is not the kind of
relationship that can be brought about quickly as trust always has
to grow, although in some circumstances it is quite remarkable how

deep a level of trust and openness can go quite quickly with an individual, or with a small group.

While Jesus never needed to confess sin he did need and value the support of an individual and a small group. John is 'the beloved disciple' precisely because there was a level of relationship which was in some way different from that held with the rest of the Twelve. Throughout the Gospels we see Jesus sometimes just sharing time with Peter, James and John (Mark 5.37; 9.2). This is most notable as Jesus goes to Gethsemane (Mark 14.32–42; Matthew 26.36–46). In his own darkest hour of temptation Jesus wanted and needed companionship. He wanted others praying with him. The three friends fell asleep but they were there.

There are times when the only way we will be able to find our way through periods of testing and temptation is through the presence and prayer of others. We have to recognize this. We have to be willing to be vulnerable in this way. If we try and battle on alone we are guaranteed to fail and fall. We need each other. God sets us in his family to help and uphold one another; as Paul put it to the Christians in Galatia, 'My friends, if anyone is detected in a transgression, you who have received the Spirit should restore such a one in a spirit of gentleness. Take care that you yourselves are not tempted. Bear one another's burdens, and in this way you will fulfil the law of Christ' (Galatians 6.1–3).

Lifelong resistance

The battle with our temptations will be with us for the whole of our lives. The types of temptation and the ways in which temptations come will in some ways change with the years but they will never go away. So the business of continually growing in knowing who we are in God and of becoming ever more secure in our identity in Christ is also lifelong. The Scriptures and prayer will need to be at the heart of our lives. We will find that we need each other just as much in our final years as in our early ones.

Relationships of deep mutual support marked by openness, honesty and vulnerability will be needed to the very end.

Ideas for reflection

1 What have you discovered of yourself as you have read through this book?
2 Take time to read a passage such as Ephesians 1.1–2.10; Romans 8; 1 Peter 1.1—2.10 or 1 John 3.1—4.21. Meditate on what these say about your identity in Christ.
3 Take one verse, such as 1 John 3.1, Galatians 2.20 or John 3.16, and meditate on it.
4 Reflect on the place of the Scriptures and prayer in your own life at present. How might this develop further?
5 With whom can you be open, honest and vulnerable about your temptations? Can others be open with you?

Pictures

Jesus Mafa: *Baptism*
Dinah Roe Kendall: *Baptism*
Sidney Spencer: *Driven by the Spirit*

Prayer

O LORD, you have searched me and known me.
For it was you who formed my inward parts;
you knit me together in my mother's womb.
I praise you, for I am fearfully and wonderfully made.
Wonderful are your works;
that I know very well.
Search me, O God, and know my heart;
test me and know my thoughts.
See if there is any wicked way in me,
and lead me in the way everlasting. Amen.

(From Psalm 139.1, 13–14, 23–24)

17

Erasing the record

————•◆•————

The stark reality of life is that time and again I do give in to temptation. I allow the first thought to develop into anger or fantasy. I give in to the desire to self-indulge by buying something further that I do not need, and justify it as retail therapy. I let the unkind word slip out. I divert the blame on to someone else. I lie. I put myself before and above God; I think I know better than he does. Or I decide not to take action to help the poor when it lies within my power to offer help. My sins are as much those of omission as commission. I am a sinner. We can all take issue with Paul when he writes, 'sinners – of whom I am the foremost' (1 Timothy 1.15) because we think that there might be some higher on the list including ourselves; but we would be very foolish to argue with him when he writes, 'all have sinned and fall short of the glory of God' (Romans 3.23). If it was down to me to resist temptation all of my life and pass the test every time then there would be no hope for me at all.

Turloch was a wild, excitable and deeply lovable young man. He delighted in winding up the children; and they responded in kind. In the early days of Longbarn camps at Carroty Woods the open field was bounded by a vast area of tall ferns. It was a wonderful setting for wide games. Every year a new cesspit had to be dug for all the waste from the chemical toilets. This was a large pit as it had to last for five weeks of 70 people. It was always dug in the ferns to hide it from view. Its position was well known and everyone took care to avoid it. The sun was shining brightly and great fun was being had by all. Some particularly scheming children had managed to wind Turloch up even higher than normal. From deep within the ferns they kept appearing and calling to him. Suddenly Turloch decided the time had come to charge and chase. He plunged forward into the tall fens without a thought. You have probably guessed by now that he ran headlong into the cesspit. The cheers rang out from the rather thoughtless children. Turloch needed help getting out of the pit. He was a very unpleasant sight, and smelt foul. All over him were bits of loo paper, the blue of the Elsan chemicals and, yes, plenty of faeces. Once such a sight is seen I promise it is never forgotten. Everyone stood their distance. Buckets of water came and were thrown over him; he was hosed down. As he pointed out later, with a mixture of shamefacedness and utter bravado, filth seemed to have got into every orifice (except thankfully his mouth which he had succeeded in keeping closed).

It is not a pleasant picture. Yet we are all rather like this. We manage to have lives covered in filth; the filth of our selfish rebellion against God. It affects, and infects, every area of our lives including our mouths (James 3.1–12). We need a thorough cleansing.

This is exactly what God does for us in Jesus Christ. He takes us as we are in all our rottenness and cleanses us from every last sin. John puts it this way, 'If we confess our sins, he who is faithful and just will forgive us our sins and cleanse us from all unrighteousness' (1 John 1.9). Paul describes the Corinthians' experience of Christ as 'you were washed, you were sanctified, you were justified in the name of the Lord Jesus Christ and in the Spirit of our God' (1 Corinthians 6.11). Baptism is the symbolic and sacramental act of entering into Christ and being washed clean from all sins. This is why, in the early centuries of the Church, the newly baptized as they came out of the water were clothed in a white robe; this symbolized their complete cleansing in Christ.

So there is one place to which all of us have to continually return – the cross of Christ. This is why the sinless one submitted himself to the cross. This is why he had to endure, and resist the temptation to avoid the suffering and death of Calvary. His death was the only way that our sins could be forgiven totally. It was his blood being poured out for us that guaranteed our cleansing. It was his obedience that brought us new life. The resurrection proved it. By his death Jesus had dealt with sin, defeated the evil one and triumphed over death (Colossians 2.13–15). Our record of failure, where we have not resisted against temptation and failed the test, was erased by Jesus at the cross.

At the foot of the cross

When we kneel, literally or metaphorically, at the foot of the cross and contemplate again the one who hung there for us we see the final and greatest victory over temptation. The one place you and I cannot go. Many of Jesus' temptations we can, and must, learn from; ours will not be so severe or demanding – but they will be of a similar nature. We learn from his example the importance of the Scriptures, the centrality of prayer, the value of the support of others and the need to choose God's way continually. We learn from him the way of truth, of patience, of confronting evil, of grace and the way of endurance. But when it comes to his final temptation – to come down from the cross and not save the world – then he is alone, in territory that none of us can ever go into. We could not, and we need not, for Christ has gone there on our behalf.

The final lesson about temptation and testing is simply this. The cross and resurrection are our one and only hope. Because Jesus went through with the cross for us, in him, we can resist temptation, and we can grow and learn through it. But when we fail to do so, as inevitably quite regularly we will, he has won the forgiveness that we need.

Ideas for reflection

Take time to meditate on the cross of Christ. Use a holding cross, or a standing cross. Use a picture of the crucifixion (Jesus Mafa:

Crucifixion; Roualt: *Crucifixion*; the CMS Resource Pack *The Christ we Share* has a wonderful selection).

You might value some music such as J. S. Bach's *St Matthew Passion*, Adrian Snell's *The Passion* or Iona's *Book of Kells*.

Prayer

Lord Jesus Christ,
Son of God,
have mercy on me, a sinner.

References

Bell, Keith (1992, 1999), *Stanley Spencer*, London: Phaidon Press.

Common Worship Services and Prayers for the Church of England (2000), London: Church House Publishing.

Hughes, Philip Edgecombe (1977), *A Commentary on the Epistle to the Hebrews*, Grand Rapids, MI: Eerdmans.

Jesus Mafa from Vie de Jesus Mafa, 24 rue de Marechal Joffre, F78000 Versailles, France, or <www.jesusmafa.com>.

Kendall, Dinah Roe (2002), *Allegories of Heaven*, Carlisle/Downers Grove, IL: Piquant Press (text from *The Message* by Eugene Peterson).

Lane, William L. (1991), *Word Biblical Commentary. Hebrews 1–8*, Dallas, TX: Word.

Lings, George (2006), *Encounters on the Edge No. 29*, Northumbria Community.